For Those Left Behind

A Jewish Anthology of Comfort and Healing

Editors
Rabbi Dov Peretz Elkins
Anne E. Pettit

Mazo Publishers

**For Those Left Behind ~ A Jewish Anthology of
Comfort and Healing**
ISBN 978-1-936778-37-9

Copyright © 2016 Dov Peretz Elkins

Published by
Mazo Publishers
P.O. Box 10474 ~ Jacksonville, Florida 32247 USA

Chaim Mazo
P.O. Box 36084 ~ Jerusalem 91360 Israel

Website: www.mazopublishers.com
Email: mazopublishers@gmail.com
Telephone: 1-815-301-3559

In loving memory of
Dr. Azriel Eisenberg, scholar and educator
~ My teacher and friend who gave me my start as a writer ~

THE EDITORS

Rabbi Dov Peretz Elkins is an internationally-known speaker and author, Rabbi Emeritus of the Jewish Center of Princeton, NJ. He coauthored *Chicken Soup for the Jewish Soul*, among his forty books and hundreds of published articles. His most recent books are *Heart and Scroll: Heartfelt Stories from the Masters, Jewish Stories from Heaven and Earth, Simple Actions for Jews to Help Green the Planet,* and *In The Spirit: Insights for Spiritual Renewal in the 21ˢᵗ Century.* He lives in Jerusalem with his wife Maxine. His website is www.JewishGrowth.org.

◆◆◆

Anne E. Pettit graduated from Columbia University with a major in Russian Studies and received a J.D. from Fordham University School of Law. After a decade as a practicing attorney, she attended and graduated from the Drisha Institute's Scholars Circle. She has taught Talmud and other Jewish subjects there and in other settings. She is a contributing editor of the e-Newsletter DOV-ray Torah. She lives in New Jersey with her husband Marc.

◆◆◆

There is a crack, a crack in everything,
That's how the light gets in.

Leonard Cohen, "Anthem"

CONTENTS

GLOSSARY

(Many of these Hebrew words and abbreviations are interspersed in the upcoming sections of this book.)

Gan Eden – Garden of Eden.
Gehinom – The Jewish concept of Hell or Purgatory; the spiritual realm in which souls are cleansed.
Goses / Goseset – Dying person.

Halakhah – Jewish Law.
Hevra Kadisha – The synagogue funeral and burial committee.
Heshbon Nefesh – Inner reckoning.

Kaddish Yatom – Mourner's Kaddish; The prayer said by a mourner in a minyan during the mourning period, and on the Yahrzeit.
Kapparah – Atonement for one's sins.
Kittel – A white robe worn by many Jewish men on Rosh Hashana and Yom Kippur; a reminder of one's mortality on these auspicious days.
Kriah – The ritual of tearing an article of clothing immediately before the funeral.

Levayah – The funeral service.

Ma'ariv (Arvit) – The evening prayer service. (See *Shacharit.*)
Mincha – The afternoon prayer service.
Mitzvot – Good deeds.

Neshama – The soul.

Olam Ha-emet – The world of truth.
Olam Ha-zeh – This world.
Olam Ha-bah – The next world.

Shacharit – The morning prayer service.

Sheloshim – The thirty-day period of mourning after a person's death.

Shiva – The seven-day mourning period after a person's death. (Also Sitting Shiva).

Taharah – The ritual washing of the body and putting on of the burial shrouds in preparation for burial, done by the *Hevra Kadisha*.

Tefilah – Prayer.

Teshuvah – Repentance.

Tikkun – Fixing or Rectifying.

Tzedakah – Charity; also acts of kindness.

Viddui – The Confessional prayer said when death appears to be close.

Yahrzeit – The memorial date.

Yerusha – Inheritance.

Yizkor – Memorial prayers recited on Yom Kippur, Simchat Torah, Pesach, and Shavuot.

ABBREVIATIONS

A.H. – *Alav ha-shalom (aleha ha-shalom)* – May peace be upon him / her. Also *olov ha-sholom.*

H.Y.D. – *Hashem yinkom damo (dama)* – May Hashem avenge his / her blood. (For martyred Jews or Jews killed by anti-Semites.)

Z.L.– *Zichrono livracha (zichronah livracha)* – of blessed memory; also, may his / her memory be a blessing. (For a non-rabbinical person.)

Z.T.L. or Z.Tz.L. – *Zecher tzadik livrakha* – may the memory of the righteous be a blessing. (For a rabbinical / righteous person.)

♦♦♦

To everything there is a season,

    And a time for every purpose under heaven.

A time to give birth, and a time to die;

    A time to plant, and a time to uproot;

A time to kill, and a time to heal;

    A time to tear down, and a time to build;

A time to weep, and a time to laugh;

    A time to mourn, and a time to dance;

A time to scatter stones and a time to gather stones;

    A time to embrace, and a time to withhold embraces;

A time to seek, and a time to lose;

    A time to guard, and a time to cast away;

A time to tear, and a time to sew together;

    A time to be silent, and a time to speak;

A time to love, and a time to hate;

    A time for war, and a time for peace.

-Ecclesiastes 3:1-8

INTRODUCTION

When sorrow and grief knock on our door, we are rarely prepared. Yet there is no creature born of woman who can avoid it.

It is the lot of everyone who walks the earth, at one time or another, to meet the dark angel face to face, and suffer the results of such an unwanted encounter.

The ninetieth Psalm in Scripture knew of this ubiquitous reality millennia ago. "You return humans to dust; You stated, 'Return O mortals ... You engulf us in sleep ... We are consumed by Your anger.'"

So much of the beautiful poetry in the Psalter returns to this constant challenge – the brevity of life, the sorrow of those left behind, the fear of everyone who comes closer to death every day that passes.

When the dark shadow falls on our home, or on our community, we grasp for support from many places. From those who share our grief – fellow travelers in the journey through the valley; from the memories in our hearts and in our photo albums, from the mementos sitting proudly on the coffee table or the mantel; from the feeling of satisfaction for what our loved ones have achieved; and from the kind words we shared when we could, whether we were aware that death was near or far.

Visitors to a house of mourning more often than not err on the side of trying too hard. Well-meaning, they often try to "cheer up" those who have suffered a loss, or distract them, thinking that this will alleviate, or postpone, the pain. But the pain is like a bodily attack, and needs to be healed in a slow, delicate way. It will not be brushed away or pushed aside. It will not be wiped clean like a slate, or a rubber eraser on paper. It is a lesion that must cure itself with the God-given modes of healing that we are heir to as humans.

We need to talk about our loved one, air our wound, not hide it under a bandage of false salve. The mourner needs to review the memories, talk about the deceased, laugh, cry, be angry – at them, at God, at himself. The range of human emotions must be set free to explode as they wish, in their normal course. We can facilitate that process by being good listeners, by asking the right questions: "Tell me about your loved one ... What did he/she love, hate, enjoy; what obsessions did she/he have? Who were her/his favorite actors, authors, musicians, artists; his/her closest friends? How did she/he attempt to suck out some of the marrow of life, and live deliberately, as Thoreau tried to do at Walden Pond?"

Adding to this therapeutic mix are soothing words that bring balm, the alchemy of support and love that is transmuted into a process of healing and calming. The process can take weeks, months, years – there is no set time or pattern. Each of us, created in the image of God, is an individual, and we heal according to our own timepiece, our own calendar.

One of the time-tested methods of mending hearts is through words. The right words can act like a magic potion, speeding the long, slow process of restoration ever so slightly.

We bring in this collection words chiseled out of the crucible of the pain of many hands – some from years past, others more recent, some from cavernous voids, others from lesser degrees of sorrow. All in one way or another part of the unfathomable plan of our Maker.

It is the hope of the editors that some of these soothing words can bring at least a small and temporary rising from the dark valley of the shadow. The two of us are not strangers to the life experience we are talking about. Being part of God's mix of living beings, we have suffered our own pain, overcome our own loss, and have confidence that some of the words collected here can be of help to others in the predicament in which we have found ourselves in days past.

Ultimately, words alone are not a panacea, but a contributing source of healing that will uplift a sorrowing heart, dry a tearing eye, and send a mourner on the necessary path to normal living. This is surely what our deceased loved one would want of us. And by finding some sources of comfort and consolation we hope to honor their memory in one of the only ways we mortals can do.

For Those Left Behind

A Jewish Anthology of Comfort and Healing

Chapter One

TO EVERYTHING THERE IS A SEASON: FACING MORTALITY

Humanity's days are like the grass;
Like a flower of the field one blooms.
A wind passes by and one is no more;
And one's place no longer knows him.
But the steadfastness of God is forever
Toward those who revere God.

-Psalm 103:15-17

It is coming for every one of us, and for everyone that we love. It may come today, tomorrow, or many years from now. We do not know when it will come, although a final illness may announce its imminent arrival. How then do we prepare to receive Death, and what sort of welcome should we give it? Do we welcome it as a friend, see it as a door to the next room of existence, greet it as a path to adventure? Is Death the ultimate enemy? Do we bar the doors and settle down for a siege, fight it with every weapon at our disposal? Do we fear it, seek to hide from it? Or do we pretend, child-like, that if we can't see it coming, Death will never be able to find us?

Truly, there are as many approaches to death and dying as there are humans on this earth. Each works out his or her approach to dying, whether that dying is one's own, or that of a loved one. We have almost all heard something about the stages we go through in coming to terms with mortality; the denial, anger, bargaining, depression and final acceptance, that come to each of us in different proportions.

Only one thing is sure, and that is that death is every bit as much a part of life as is birth. They are the bookends to earthly existence. Dying is also living, right up to the very end, which is also a beginning. The old advice to live every day as if it were one's last may be trite, but it is true. If we take it, no matter when Death comes for us, whether we are young or old, we will have lived the fullness of Life.

The Pattern of the Universe

Judaism ... teaches us to understand death as part of the Divine pattern of the universe. Actually, we could not have our sensitivity without fragility. Mortality is the tax that we pay for the privilege of love, thought, creative work – the toll on the bridge of being, from which clods of the earth and snow-peaked mountain summits are exempt ... We are prisoners of the years, yet that very prison is the room of discipline in which we, driven by the urgency of time, create.

Actually, there could be no growth, no progress, if generations did not come and go ... There is a time to run gaily with all the intense excitement of a boy with flushed cheeks racing on a summer's day toward the winding river of sport and adventure; there is also the time when that boy, transformed by the alchemy of the years into an old man, no longer seeks to run but it is quite content to sit and browse even unto the twilight.

-Rabbi Joshua Loth Liebman

Fear Not Death

If we can succeed in accepting the inexorable fact of our own death with equanimity, perhaps it will mitigate our sorrow over the death of a loved one. We can even learn to regard death not as an enemy but as a friend, who at the appointed hour leads us like Longfellow's little child at bedtime "half willing half reluctant to be led." Sancho Panza in *Don Quixote* spends a desperate night clinging to a window ledge, afraid of falling. When day breaks, he discovers that all the while his feet had been only an inch from the ground. Our fear of death may be as groundless as Sancho's fear of falling. Death may be but the threshold over which we pass from time to eternity; from the realm of the perishable to the realm of the indestructible. And if we come to terms with death, who would dare to set a limit on what we could extract from life?

-Rabbi Sidney Greenberg

A Saying by Black Elk

A book of Native American wisdom: a saying by Black Elk (1770-1853), the chief of the Omaha Native Americans. Black Elk lived at a time of hardship and transition for his tribe. Foreigners threatened to take his land, and the Sioux were a warring tribe against his. But the biggest danger he faced was small pox, which had come to America via Europeans and was a rampant cause of death among Native Americans. Black Elk needed to give his people a sense of hope and perspective on managing a difficult past and having strength to face the future. Here is what he told his tribe:

"Do not grieve. Misfortunes will happen to the wisest and best of men. Death will come, always out of season. It is the command of the Great Spirit, and all the nations and people must obey. What is past and what cannot be prevented should not be grieved for ... Misfortunes do not flourish particularly in our lives – they grow everywhere."

Not Just Today, But Every Day

Rabbi Eliezer said: "Repent one day before your death."

His disciples asked: "Does anyone know on what day he will die?"

"All the more reason to repent today," answered the Rabbi, "in case you die tomorrow. Thus a person's whole life should be spent in repentance."

-Babylonian Talmud, Shabbat, 153A

A Modern Version of *Viddui* – the Confessional Before Dying

"I am sending an angel before you to guard
you on the way and to bring you to the place
I have made ready"

-Exodus 23:20

The *viddui* (confessional) is traditionally recited when a person is at the point of death. It is important to stress that the *viddui* in no way requires or encourages the loss of hope or the will to live (Shulhan Arukh Yoreh De'ah 338:1). It is intended to comfort the dying person (*goses/goseset*) and lovingly address and ease any fears, guilt, or anxiety. The *viddui* offers an opportunity to say goodbye, and according to traditional Rabbinic understanding, to make one's death a holy moment and a *kapparah* (atonement for one's sins).

> My Source, God of those who came before me: I know that my cure and my death are in Your hands. May You heal me completely, move me to wholeness. But if death is nearing, I am ready to receive it from your hand.
>
> May all the wrongdoings I have done in my life – those things I have done unwittingly, those things I have done knowingly; acts I have done to myself, to others, to You – may they all be forgiven.
>
> Allow the hidden goodness stored for *tzaddikim* (the righteous) to flow over me. Help me to understand the path of life. Gift me continuing life in the hidden world yet to come.
>
> As I come close to You now, Your face bathes me with light. Being at Your right hand fills me deeply.
>
> One who watches over the vulnerable and needy, take care of my close ones, those precious ones with whom my soul is intertwined.

Shema Yisra'el Adonai Elo'heinu Adonai Ehad
Listen, Israel, our God, our Source, is one.

-Rabbi Vicky Hollander

Get A Life

I am madly addicted to reading Personal Ads. They tell you a lot about what people are looking for in their lives. But this past summer, I found an ad in the *Berkshire Advocate*. The woman was not looking for a relationship. Or maybe she was. Maybe she was looking for a relationship ... that goes beyond relationships.

> *"I am a 58 year old woman with, doctors tell me, one year to live. I would like to spend that year doing something meaningful, interesting, and fun. I like C-span, Bill Moyers, Times crosswords, Nina Totenberg, Anna Quindlan, Mario Cuomo, Nevada. I don't like George Will, R.J. Reynolds, computer talk fundamentalists, California. I have limited stamina and resources. Have you any ideas how I can spend this year making a difference?"*

I do not know if the woman is Jewish or not. But she managed to condense the entire Yom Kippur liturgy into eight lines in the back of a free weekly newspaper. "For what is our life, and what our vaunted strength? What can we say in Your presence?" She has re-written the *Unetaneh Tokef,* asking in the pages of the *Advocate* what in our world might temper the Decree over which we have no control. This is the great, unspoken theme of Yom Kippur. It is why we fast. It is why we wear white. It is why tomorrow we will read of Jonah's sojourn in the belly of the whale. On Yom Kippur, we confront our own mortality. There is only one difference between the woman in the *Berkshire Advocate* and us. She gave voice to what we already, deep down in our hearts, know to be true.

-Rabbi Jeffrey Salkin

Who Shall Live and Who Shall Die?
Who in the Fullness of Years, and Who Not?

It was the first pulpit Rabbi Cynthia Culpeper ever had – Montgomery, Alabama's Agudath Israel Synagogue, where she began her rabbinic service in the summer of 1995. She had been a Registered Nurse at San Francisco General Hospital, and decided to return to rabbinical school. Her excitement knew no bounds when she was ordained and then called to serve as spiritual leader in her own congregation in Alabama.

Shortly before Rosh Hashanah she went to have a sore throat checked. The day after Rosh Hashanah she was told that she was HIV-positive, and two weeks after that she was diagnosed with AIDS. She immediately informed her congregation. In January 1994 she received an "occupational exposure" at the hospital where she served, and was tested twice within the year following, both times negative. Now, shortly after the High Holy Days, she was given a death sentence. In her letter to her congregation she wrote: "You can well imagine how intense Yom Kippur was for me this year, my first as a rabbi at that. Its unending primary liturgical message of how our lives are in the balance took on a whole new meaning for me."

In so many ways the *Unetaneh Tokef* prayer still resonates for each of us as we stare fate in the eye and wonder what the future will bring for us. There is no clear answer in the prayer, but only the hope that through *Teshuvah*, *Tefilah* and *Tzedakah* – through Repentance, Prayer and Acts of Kindness – we can make our lives meaningful, whether we have one year or eight years left on this earth.

-D.P.E.

Soaring to Greater Heights

(Ari L. Goldman, former religion writer for The New York Times, wrote a touching memoir on his father's death, called Living A Year Of Kaddish, in which he reminisces about the year after his father's passing, and the death of other members of his family. Here are his words:)

Soon after I returned to New York, I got word that my forty-six-year-old cousin Elise Goldman was terminally ill with cancer. Elise, who grew up in Hartford, lived in Florida with her husband, Murray, and their ten-year-old daughter, Shanna. Elise died in late March and the family assembled to bid her farewell a few days later in a cemetery in Woodbridge, New Jersey. I saw a lot of Elise when we were children, but had lost contact with her over the years. I had never met Shanna, but knew who she was right away when I saw her at the funeral.

With big hopeful eyes, a ready smile, and a head of curly black hair, she looked just like her mother.

The family on my father's side is a large one; I am one of fourteen grandchildren of Sam and Nettie Goldman. My cousins and I had gathered before at other family funerals and memorial services, but this one was different. This funeral was for one of our own. Elise was the first of our generation to die.

But as we gathered in sorrow and in pain, we were surprised to find that it was Elise who was concerned about us. Before she died, she penned these words, which were read by our cousin Donna at the funeral: "I feel badly about the pain I have caused through my passing, and yet I could not have waited any longer. I know what awaits me and it is wonderful. In the twilight of death between this world and the next, I could get brief glimpses."

She wrote that she did not fear death and implored us not to grieve. "Remember me with joy and health, and rejoice with me that I am whole again and need not suffer anymore." As we heard her words, it was almost as if she were standing beside us at her open grave. "When you bury me," Donna read, "do not imagine me below the earth, but above it, soaring to greater heights on the wings of those who have gone before and return to help me make my journey from the darkness to the light.

> "May your pain be healed in God's light as he has healed mine. I love you all, now and forever."

> -Ari L. Goldman

A Holy Place

I still remember one of my first experiences with death, which occurred very early in my work as a chaplain. I was on call at the hospital when I was asked to be with a family whose loved one was dying in the intensive care unit (ICU). Life support had been disconnected; there was nothing to do but wait for death. Family members gathered around the death bed, the eerie sounds of the ICU in the background, as they held a vigil for the woman who was wife, mother and grandmother. The vigil, as it turned out, went on for some hours. I spent time with the family and then went to visit with other hospital patients, checking back from time to time. I remember little about what was said during that time. What I remember most is the silence, the hush, the sensation of our watching the monitors together. Finally, the line on the heart monitor went flat. There were tears and prayers, and a bit of relief. Most of all, I remember the sense of awe, the awareness that we had all stood in a holy place.

-Rabbi Amy Eilberg

Is It Really The End?

Is it really the end? The path is still clear.
The mists of life still beckon from afar
The sky is still blue, the grass green;
Autumn is coming.

I shall accept the judgment.
My heart harbors no complaint.
How red were my sunsets,
How clear my dawns!
And flowers smiled along my path
As I passed.

-Rachel (trans. Rabbi Sidney Greenberg)

Fifteen-Year-Old Teaches Lessons About Living and Dying

The obituary page of the New York Times on April 30, 1994 told of the death of a fifteen-year-old boy named Joseph Lopez, Jr. It read as follows:

"Joseph Luis Lopez, Jr., a co-author of *I Will Sing Life: Voice From the Hole in the Wall,* an award-winning book by and about children with life-threatening medical problems, died on Thursday at his family home in Jersey City, NJ. He was 15."

The obituary goes on to explain that Joseph died of AIDS, after being in a coma for 2 weeks. He liked to call himself Joe Louis Lopez, after the famous boxer, Joe Louis. Joseph had been HIV positive since birth. The medical director of a camp where Joseph went in the summer, called Hole in the Wall Gang Camp, for children with cancer and other life-threatening diseases in Ashford, CT, and a professor of pediatrics at Yale Medical School, said that "Joe was a fighter and was fighting for life really up until the very end."

Joe collaborated on the 200-page book during the three summers he was at the camp. It was published by Little, Brown in 1992, with six other campers, ages 7 to 19, and with two camp counselors, Larry Berger and Dahlia Lithwick.

Joe says in the book: "HIV is nothing. It's just a virus. It's just like being sick for a long time, for always. I say, put on your gloves and fight 'em, go 10 rounds. You have to beat it. But some people, they're scared, they just say, 'Nah, I can't beat it, I can't.' They don't care about themselves because they think they're dying. I got nothing to talk about dying. I ain't dying yet."

The introduction to Joe's book was written by actor Paul Newman, the camp's founder and president. The book won awards from the New York Public Library and the National Association for the Care of Children's Health. It has also been published in Denmark and Germany. Joseph's mother, who passed the virus to her son at birth, died in 1986.

I think the facts speak for themselves. No further comment is necessary.

-D.P.E.

Voice of the Soul

The call came at noon. My mother, a strong and vivacious woman in her early 70s, was being rushed to an emergency room with acute abdominal pain. I was half a continent away and after frantic phone calls, finally got through to her doctor who felt that she had developed an acute intestinal obstruction and that he was calling in a surgeon. Within 20 minutes, the surgeon called in to say that she would have to undergo an exploratory surgery. However, her condition had deteriorated so rapidly and she was nearly in shock.

"I'm going to put her in the unit and try and get her a little more stable before we go to the O.R." Then, after a brief pause, he said in a low voice, "I think you'd better come." The meaning of that statement was poignantly clear to me, and there was a deep sinking feeling in the pit of my stomach.

The next few hours were a whirlwind of activity, canceling clinics, arranging coverage, and trying to get a flight. As I threw some things together into my briefcase, one of my colleagues handed me a portable CD player with some CDs. "Take it along, it might make the waiting easier." Muttering a half-hearted thanks, I shoved it into my bag and sped off to the airport.

The only flight I could get on such short notice required a connection through Pittsburgh. On the way to the airport I called the hospital, only to hear my father's tearful voice telling me that they were taking my mother to the operating room. I hurried onto the plane as a heavy rain mixed with sleet began to fall.

Upon arriving in Pittsburgh, I rushed to make my connection only to be told that the fog and the rain had delayed all flights. Cursing, I tried to call the hospital but could not get through to anyone. An overwhelming sense of despair came over me, and I slumped into a hard chair in a dark corner of the airport. Normally, when I travel I take along work to catch up on, journals to look at, and a dictating recorder to catch up on correspondence. But, I could do nothing as I sat, feeling overwhelmed by a sense of utter hopelessness.

After a time, I noticed the edge of the disc player sticking out of my briefcase. Absentmindedly, I opened it and found it containing a single CD set, the Mahler Symphony No. 9. There, alone in a dark corner, my thought a thousand miles away, I put on the headset and pressed play. Suddenly, it was as if I heard music for the very first time. From the first notes onward I was transfixed, my deep emotional stress breaking down any barrier between myself and the music. I heard it as Mahler had meant it – a message of farewell, of the acceptance of mortality, and the profound realization of how precious life is in the very moment it seems most fragile. Written after the death of his beloved daughter, when he himself was dying of rheumatic heart disease, it stands as a testament to the ebbing of a great man's life, and is one of the greatest pieces of music ever composed.

-Blair P. Grubb, MD

Requiem

Under the wide and starry sky,
Dig the grave and let me die.
Glad did I live and gladly die,
And I laid me down with a will.

This be the verse you grave for me:
Here he lies where he longed to be;
Home is the sailor, home from the sea,
And the hunter home from the hill.

-Robert Louis Stevenson

To What End?

There is no teacher like mourning. Now that death has come close to me, both by taking the man I once loved and then by almost taking me, I am not the person I was before. I can only describe the change in most personal terms. I am so glad to be alive, so grateful that my parents are alive and healthy, so thankful that I went on to love another man and make such an interesting and enjoyable life with him. I am richly blessed to live in a loving community in a beautiful place.

Yet , it could all go in a minute. It *will* all go in a minute. This life is a brief stop, whether I die tomorrow or in fifty years. I would love not to know this, to have the innocent certainty that, when loved ones set out on a journey, they will return unharmed, that I can go out to sea in my boat, play in the waves and not be swallowed up. But I am more grateful now than I ever was in my innocence.

In the end it is all a gift, is it not? The brief entwinement of body and soul, the breath of God that gives and sustains human life, creates such a colorful, sparkling trail as it arcs through time. It is so ephemeral, and yet it affects everything. As we say when we open our eyes every morning: "I give thanks to You, God of life who is eternal, for returning my soul to me this morning. Great is Your faithfulness."

-Rabbi Margaret Holub

Reflections Upon the New Year

The same God that made Moses made me, made you, and He made us for a brief time. So let us not depend upon others to do the work in this world. Let us not give our lives away. It is a profound tradition that begins the new year by reminding us of death. But it is only by acknowledging death that we understand the inestimable, the incalculable value of our own lives.

Only that is precious which passes away. Only that is priceless which will not last forever, and we will not last forever. By facing death we are spurred to life. The year to come will bring death. That is the inescapable certainty that haunts us each Rosh Hashanah and Yom Kippur. Some whom many of us knew who were with us last year are no longer with us. We can be certain that next year too will bring in tragedies. The next year will bring the gradual ebbing of our powers, and the sudden, unfair catastrophe of death. The question which each of us must answer in the hidden chambers of our souls and our hearts is simply this: knowing that next year will bring death, will we fill our days with the force, the promise, and power of life?

-Rabbi David J. Wolpe

Notice You're Alive

On this solemn day Orthodox men wear a white shroud called a *"kittel."* This is the same garment they will wear when they are buried. It gets you used to the idea that there is an end to becoming. If you want to live a spiritual life the task is to do it now. A portion of the Yom Kippur ritual is called "Yizkor." This is a memorial service for those who have passed on. Jews are obligated to attend this service to remember their dead relatives. Even if you are not a member of a congregation, the doors are open – no one is ever turned away from performing this holy task of honoring one's relatives. (You can understand the enormous security concerns synagogues had this year with talk of terror, retribution and war).

Just days before the Yizkor service I happened to read a newspaper interview with Warren Zevon. He is a singer/

songwriter with a piercing wit and dark humor. Warren had just been diagnosed with inoperable lung cancer. In the interview he said he was not expecting a miracle – "It's been made abundantly clear to me that the recovery statistic of what I have is zero."

A thirty-year smoker, Warren said bitterness and regret had no role in his current thinking. He did acknowledge that he'd rather have been told he had the flu. He also said that he'd certainly like to tell someone, "Look, if you don't want to die at 55 you might not want to smoke for thirty years; but this is my life and these were my choices." He hoped his kids would make better ones.

Warren said he was grateful for everything he had and that his diagnosis reaffirmed his philosophy "Notice You're Alive". He said this was his life's message and what his songs were about; enjoy life, make the most of every word, every poem and every flower. Warren noticed his aliveness now with an intensity he never appreciated before.

It seems to me that's what Yom Kippur and the *"kittel"* is all about: Take some time to ask yourself if your life accurately reflects your beliefs. Is your life an example of your message? The days go by too quickly, this is the time to notice how alive you are. Change that which keeps you from living your truth and together we can change the world before the book is closed.

-Carl A. Hammerschlag, MD

Entering the Real World

The Hebrew word for coffin is *Aron*. Aron is the same word that is used for the Holy Ark in which a Sefer Torah is housed. And it is used in another place in the Torah. When Noah builds a floating house in which to bring his family when the flood is coming, the Torah calls it an *"Aron."* So the Torah's Ark is called an *"Aron,"* just as the Holy Ark in the Sanctuary, and the floating house which Noah built. The coffin is an *"Aron"* because, like the Holy Ark that contains the *Sefer Torah*, that which it contains is holy. It holds the remains of a holy being for all time.

The *Aron* that holds the remains of a holy person is very

small. There just enough room for the person inside. Not enough room for anything but the good deeds done in this world. There is no need and no room for stocks or bonds or cash or bank accounts – these can't be used in the world where our loved ones go after death.

Maybe that's why our Tradition uses the same word for a coffin, a synagogue Ark, and Noah's floating house. And for one more reason: In some Jewish communities it is the custom to drill a hole in the bottom of the coffin to hasten the return from dust to dust.

Rabbi James Ponet once wrote: Even the final "home" is not so much a sanctuary *from* the world, as an entrance into it. Let's think of our loved ones as having entered the *real* world – the world of truth – *Olam Ha-emet.*

-Adapted from Rabbi Jack Riemer and Rabbi James Ponet

Nothing to Fear

The perspective on death is exemplified by an incident that occurred with Rabbi Yosef Yitzchak of Lubavitch, who defied the order of the Russian government that he cease and desist preaching and teaching Judaism.

A Russian officer confronted Rabbi Yosef Yitzchak and pulled his gun on him, but the Rabbi did not flinch.

"Are you not afraid that I can kill you?" the officer asked.

The Rabbi replied, "One who has a multiplicity of gods and only one world is frightened of dying. Those who have only one God and two worlds have no fear of death."

When my father was diagnosed with cancer of the pancreas, he showed no signs of anxiety. He then told me that just a few weeks earlier his father had appeared to him in a dream and said, "There is nothing to fear. It is just walking out of one room and walking into another." My father said, "I knew then that my life was coming to an end, and I was only waiting to discover how this was to come about."

-Rabbi Abraham J. Twerski

The Fire in our Lives

Early in the century, naturalists who cared for the great sequoias of Yosemite were careful to avoid fires. They did not realize the function of fire in the eco-system. Periodic burning clears the brush and ensures that huge fires do not break out. Fire also clears space for the sun to reach the forest floor and foster new growth. In preventing small fires, giant fires broke out, destroying sections of the forest that are only now reaching equilibrium.

For the trees saved by the policy of preventing fires, the policy was wonderful. But it threatened, in time, to engulf the forest.

Death is the fire that consumes our lives. Without it there would be no space for new growth. The world would be choked. On an individual level, however, it is hard to avoid the feeling of the tree that is spared.

All creation necessitates limitation: the picture its frame, the story its denouement, the life its death. Do we argue for the necessity of death because we are confronted by its inevitability? Would we design the world with death if we were beginning anew? The midrash teaches that when God called creation "very good" the phrase referred to death. Judaism teaches us both to cherish life and to understand the inevitability of death. A paradox, like the beneficent fire in the forest.

-Rabbi David Wolpe

Do We Want an Immortal World?

The late Rabbi Ben-Zion Bokser gave an inspired illustration that puts death into a helpful perspective. To someone who expressed a grudge against God for taking the life of his close friend, a truly righteous man who deserved to live forever, God appeared in a dream and demonstrated what life would be like if, indeed, all nature survived forever.

God placed him in an immortal world where not a flower faded nor a blossom withered. Summer came and went, but nothing changed one iota. The crowning glory of nature in full summer bloom, with its rich and varied hues and the majestic beauty and power of its intertwining stems, leaves and flowers, took on a fixed permanence. Perfection was preserved for all eternity; life was rendered permanently immune to the ravages of time.

For a while the dreamer placed into this situation was thrilled by it all, until the realization dawned that this static state meant that although nothing grew old, decayed, or died, nothing was born either! Though spared the sadness of witnessing decline and death, he could not look forward with eager expectation, nor observe with rewarding fascination, the birth of new life and its growth and development, and the marvels of the ever-changing face of God's earth and human society.

The dreamer soon tired of the sameness of everything: the same shapes, sizes, formations, and colors. He longed to witness, enjoy, and be inspired by the evolution of new plant, animal, and especially human, life. And when he awoke from his dream he was content to surrender the bittersweet gift of immortality, appreciating full well that the heady experience of even a limited life span–albeit with death as its sad though inevitable climax–was still far preferable to the boring immutability that was its alternative.

-D.P.E.

Dying a Good Death

Perhaps one of the greatest of human tragedies is when a person who has lived a fine and upright life turns to evil in the twilight of his days. The Talmud tells the story of a greatly respected High Priest, who ministered to the Jewish People for decades. Tragically, in the final years of his life, he came to deny the truth of God and Torah.

In light of this, the Talmud advises that "everyone should repent the day before he dies." Obviously, since no one knows when his day of death will be, the Talmud is recommending to set aside time every day to ponder one's actions. In fact, Jews recite a prayer three times a day asking God for help in repairing our misdeeds.

Many religious figures have stressed the importance of "dying a good death." A beautiful example is found in [the]

Torah portion, Pinchas.

In the *Parashah*, Moses is told by God to prepare to die. Moses' life had been characterized, perhaps more than anything else, by his great dedication to the Jewish people. Time and time again, he went through great travail and turmoil to help them.

Faced with the news that his demise is imminent, Moses – surprisingly – does not ask for a longer life. Instead, his immediate response is to ask God to ensure that the Jewish people are blessed with a proper leader. He prays that the nation should not be like a "flock without a shepherd." Moses' dedication to the people is so great, that he is concerned only with their welfare – even when faced with the specter of his own death.

The commentaries point out the unusual way in which Moses addresses God. Moses refers to the "God of the Spirits," an appellation that is rarely used in Jewish tradition. Rashi explains that the "spirits" referred to here are the souls of the individual Israelites. Moses was alluding to the aspect of God that is sensitive to the needs of each individual. This is the Name of God that Moses invoked when praying that the new leader of Israel should take care of each and every Jew.

Both in life and death, Moses showed himself to be totally at one with his people.

This genuine concern for each individual has become the hallmark of Jewish leadership throughout the centuries. The Talmud in particular, stresses that a leader must understand how everyone has his or her own particular view of reality. The leader must be able to rise above all pettiness – and become the umbrella which both encompasses and protects everyone.

Moses was a master of this. In fact, the Kabbalah (Jewish mysticism) drives home this point by declaring that "every Jew has a little piece of Moses in him."

The Shlah, a great mystic and Biblical commentator, explains that only the Messiah will equal Moses in his compassion for (and understanding of) each and every Jew. May we merit such leadership, soon in our days.

-Rabbi Yehuda Appel

Life Is Fragile

Rabbi David Wolpe tells the story of when his baby girl was born, and he had someone come to child-proof his home. He and his wife engaged a professional "house-proofer" to come and put soft pads on all the rough edges of the square tables, locks on all the silverware drawers and cabinets where cleaning detergents and medicines might be, etc. etc.

At the end of the day-long process, the man gave him a bill for a huge sum of money. Rabbi Wolpe couldn't believe the amount of money he was paying for this service, important as it was.

But the kicker was that as he was leaving, the "house-proofer" turned to him and said: Now, the most important thing is this: Don't take your eyes off of her!

The lesson is that we often think that we can do things to stave off evil and harm, and even death. In the *Unetaneh Tokef* prayer, we talk about living and dying, and shudder at the thought that we all must eventually die. Everything we do on Yom Kippur has to do with reminding us of our ultimate demise. We wear a *kittel*, resembling a shroud. We fast, because those who have passed on have no need to eat.

Rabbi Wolpe was reminded that we can try our best to prolong life, and try to prevent harm and pain from coming to those whom we love, but in the last analysis, we are all vulnerable, mortal, and finite – and our efforts are worthy, but never completely successful.

-D.P.E.

Death on Shabbat

Someone born on Shabbos will die on Shabbos, since the great day of the Shabbos was profaned on his account. Rava bar Rav Shila said, "And he will be called a great and holy man" (Shabbat 156a). For, dying on Shabbos is a holy thing, and not everyone is worthy of such a death. According to the Arizal, one who dies on Shabbos does so free of sin.

-Rabbi Pinchas Winston

Verses for Contemplation

Short, alas, is the life of man, limited and fleeting, full of pain and torment. One should wisely understand this, do good deeds and lead a holy life, for no mortals ever escape death.

Just as the dewdrop, at the point of the grassblade at sunrise, very soon vanishes and does not remain for long: just so is the dew drop-like life of men very short and fleeting.

Just as at the pouring down of a mighty rain, the bubbles on the water very soon vanish and do not remain for long: just so is the bubble-like life of men very short and fleeting.

Just as a furrow drawn with a stick in the water very soon vanishes and does not remain for long: just so is the furrow-like life of men very short and fleeting.

Just as the cattle for slaughter, whatever their footing, stand on the brink of death: just so is the life of men very short and fleeting.

One should wisely understand this, do good deeds and lead a holy life, for no mortal ever escapes death.

-The Buddha, Anguttara Nikaya

When Thou Callest Me

God, Thou hast gifted me with blessings beyond my merit and hast shielded me times without number from evil and hurt. Thou hast guided me through many years of life and hast caused it to be enriched by the love dear ones have given to me. Thou hast enabled me to serve my fellowmen and my community and hast not withheld from me evidence of the regard and friendship in which others have held me. Thou hast set my lot in a land of freedom and justice and Hast spared me the indignities and torments which so many of my brethren have endured.

O God of truth and mercy, it is in disregard of the many rich bounties Thou hast showered upon me that I approach Thee for yet another manifestation of Thy infinite and divine love, Thou who hast made me in the past the object of Thy care and concern, grant me one more plea.

O God, when in Thy wisdom Thou callest me to leave this

earthly life I shall come uncomplaining and unafraid, since it is Thou who calls. But let Thy command that I depart this life be sharp, clear, and decisive. Remove me, O God, quickly and do not let me journey with lingering slowness and halting steps from life here to withersoever Thou wouldst lead me. Spare me a long interval of helplessness, the delaying period of a low illness before my breath ceases in fulfillment of Thy wish. Allow me, O God, to leave in instantaneous compliance with Thy decree and bestow upon all whom I love that healing solace which Thou alone canst give. May but a quickly passing moment separate life from death so that I may serve Thee in whatever realm awaits me, with unimpaired strength of body and vigor of mine. Take me unto Thee, O Father, in wholeness, not broken and wracked by suffering and illness: Graciously grant me the great joy of coming to Thee with reverent gratitude for Thy many blessings in this life and with unfaltering trust and faith in the life beyond, to which Thou hast summoned me. Amen!

-Rabbi Morris Adler

Just In Time

Novelist Vicki Baum once said, "You don't get ulcers from what you eat. You get them from what's eating you." And what's eating us much of the time is worry. It eats us from the inside out.

I wish I could always be like former baseball player Mickey Rivers. He philosophized, "Ain't no sense worrying about things you got control over, because if you got control over them, ain't no sense worrying. And there ain't no sense worrying about things you got no control over either, because if you got no control them, ain't no sense worrying."

Maybe that makes sense, I'm just not sure. But even if it does, I'll likely wind up worried anyway. Which is why I like this story related by inspirational Dutch author and holocaust survivor Corrie ten Boom.

Corrie learned a powerful lesson as a little girl. Having encountered the lifeless body of a baby, she realized that people she loved would someday die, too. She thought about the fact that her father and mother and sister Betsie could quite possibly pass on before she did. The thought frightened and worried her.

One night her father came in to tuck her into bed. Corrie burst into tears and sobbed, "I need you. You can't die. You can't!"

Her father sat on the edge of the narrow bed and spoke tenderly to his daughter. "Corrie," he said gently, "when you and I go to Amsterdam, when do I give you your ticket?"

She sniffed a few times and considered the question. "Why, just before I get on the train," she answered.

"Exactly," he continued. Then he gave her assurance that was to last a lifetime. "When the time comes that some of us have to die, you will look into your heart and find the strength you need – just in time."

Some years later Corrie and her family, arrested for sheltering Jews and members of the Dutch resistance, were sent to Nazi concentration camps. She, indeed, experienced the deaths of her parents and sister, as well as numerous friends. She endured hardships that she could never have imagined as a young child. But the words of her father stayed with her and proved to be true. "You will look into your heart and find the strength you need – just in time." She always did. Regardless of the suffering or hardship she encountered, when she looked inside her heart she found the strength she needed – just in time.

If you worry and fret, or if you feel anxious about your future, you may find Corrie's experience helpful. And if that thing you dread should ever arrive, then you need only look inside your heart. The strength you need can be found there – just in time.

-Steve Goodier

When Death Comes

When death comes like the hungry bear in autumn ...

When death comes and takes all the bright coins from his purse to buy me, and snaps his purse shut ...

When death comes like the measle-pox ...

When death comes like an iceberg
between the shoulder blades ...

I want to step through the door full of curiosity, wondering ...
what is it going to be like ...
that cottage of darkness?

And therefore I look upon everything as
a brotherhood and a sisterhood ...

And I look upon time as no more than an idea,
and I consider eternity as another possibility ...

And I think of each life as a flower,
as common as a field daisy, and as singular ...

And each name a comfortable music in the mouth
tending as all music does, toward silence ...

And each body a lion of courage, and something
precious to the earth.

When it's over, I want to say ...
all my life
I was a bride, married to amazement.
I was a bridegroom, taking the world into my arms.

When it's over ...
I don't want to wonder
if I have made of my life something particular, and real.
I don't want to find myself sighing and frightened
or full of argument.

I don't want to end up ...
simply having visited this world.

-Mary Oliver

Chapter Two

ONE STEP AT A TIME: THE JOURNEY THROUGH GRIEF

A famous Zen master had died. One of his students, a young monk, was grief stricken, crying inconsolably. His friend, another young monk, came up to him and said, "Why are you crying? We have learned so much about impermanence, about death not being final. Why are you crying?" With clarity, the young monk looked at him and replied, "I am crying because I am sad, you fool!"

When a close relative dies, Jews rend a piece of clothing. The resulting tear is the perfect metaphor for the experience of grief – a vital piece of our world has been torn away; our very souls have been ripped. Neither the article of clothing nor our hearts will ever be the same again. There is no going back; no matter how skillful the seamstress or tailor, the fibers of the cloth will never be whole again. Nor will the fibers of our hearts.

Grief comes with stages of its own. From the first, cruel pain of loss, through the dull ache punctuated with sharper pain (the first anniversary without a spouse; the first Seder without Zayde or Bubbe; the joy of a child's birth dampened by the absence of a beloved family member), and finally, the bittersweet weaving of the memory of our loved ones into life's events. He would have loved (or maybe hated) the new rabbi. How she would have enjoyed these roses. Our son, our daughter, would have been so good at this.

Perhaps grief is less an emotion than a road that must be traveled. The road passes from the new and unwanted reality of loss through fields of memory, bitter and sweet, through sun and storm to an unknown destination. We may never feel that we've reached a destination, but we finally get used to the road, and perhaps take note of others traveling it on journeys of their own. We make it part of our lives, and it serves to keep our loved ones present to us in this world even as they inhabit the next one.

And what of those who surround one who grieves? Many volumes have been written on the art and etiquette of comforting, but in the end it comes down to this: It is a great mitzvah to participate in *levayah*, escorting the dead to their places of burial. But there is levayah for the living as well, the comfort of presence that all can give along the road of grief. No repair job or therapy required. As the old saying goes, "Don't walk behind me – I may not lead. Don't walk in front of me – I may not follow. Just walk beside me, and be my friend."

The Three Ways of Mourning

There are three ways to mourn: to weep, to be silent, and to sing.

- *The first way to mourn is to weep:* even if our tears are for ourselves, for our ache of loneliness, for our pain of loss, they are still sacred, for they are the tears of love. But we may weep only if we do not weep too long, only if the spark of our own spirit is not quenched by a grief too drawn out, only if we do not indulge ourselves in the luxury of grief until it deprives us of courage and even the wish for recovery.

- *The second way to mourn is to be silent:* to behold the mystery of love, to recall a shared moment, to remember a word or a glance, or simply at some unexpected moment, to miss someone very much and wish that he or she could be here. The twinge lasts but a moment, and passes in perfect silence.

- *The third way to mourn is to sing:* to sing a hymn to life, a life that still abounds in sights and sounds and vivid colors; to sing the song our beloved no longer has the chance to sing. We sing the songs of our beloved; we aspire to their qualities of spirit; and we trust in our heart that there is a God who hears the bittersweet melody of our song.

-Hasidic

A Time For Silence

The world will not keep quiet.

Stores play music, billboards blare, our cars, iPods, and cellphones bombard us with words, images, and music. Still, silence and absence are among our most important teachers. As a great pianist once remarked, his playing uniquely was distinguished less by the notes than the space between the notes. Mystics studied not only the black letters of the Torah, but the white spaces between them. Stillness, absence, silence – the first letter of the Ten Commandments was an aleph, which has no sound.

Ecclesiastes was certainly correct that "there is a time to speak and a time to keep silent." Silence corresponds sometimes to a deep need inside of us for peace, for a brief cessation of the tumult that disguises our hunger and distracts our sadness. Even our tradition of words knows that words are not always welcome. The *Midrash* on *Kohelet* tells a story: The wife of Rabbi Mana died. Rabbi Abin came to pay a condolence call. Rabbi Mana asked, "Are there any words of Torah you would like to offer us in time of grief?" Rabbi Abin answered, "At times like this the Torah takes refuge in silence."

-Rabbi David Wolpe

No One Can Sidestep Darkness

No one can sidestep darkness. Rabbi Aharon of Apt taught that darkness is the throne upon which the light sits. If a soul has not known sadness and struggle there is no chance of overcoming, no cherishing the dawn.

-Rabbi David Wolpe

Dirge Without Music

I am not resigned to the shutting away of loving hearts
    in the hard ground.
So it is, and so it will be, for so it has been,
    time out of mind:
Into the darkness they go, the wise and the lovely.
Crowned with lilies and with laurel they go;
But I am not resigned.

Lovers and thinkers, into the earth with you.
Be one with the dull, the indiscriminate dust.
A fragment of what you felt, of what you knew,
A formula, a phrase remains,–but the best is lost.

The answers quick and keen, the honest look, the
    laughter, the love,–
They are gone.
They are gone to feed the roses.
Elegant and curled is the blossom.
Fragrant is the blossom.
I know. But I do not approve.
More precious was the light in your eyes
    than all the roses in the world.

Down, down, down into the darkness of the grave
Gently they go, the beautiful, the tender, the kind;
Quietly they go, the intelligent, the witty, the brave.
I know. But I do not approve.
And I am not resigned.

-Edna St. Vincent Millay

Keeping Our Balance in the Open Sea

Facing loss, dealing with our pain and grief, are among the most challenging and trying tasks a human being ever faced.

The late sage, Albert Einstein, wrote in a letter to friends, who had unexpectedly lost a child, on April 26, 1945:

"When the unexpected course of everyday life is interrupted, we realize that we are like shipwrecked people trying to keep their balance on a miserable plank in the open sea, having forgotten where they came from and not knowing whither they are drifting."

-The Quotable Einstein, p. 108

Why Me?

At Yizkor time people often feel that life is unfair. We are robbed of our loved ones before their time. Rarely does it happen that when someone dies their spouse or children feel that their life was long enough. There is a saying that a good life is never long enough, even if it stretches into the nineties. Somehow, ironically, the longer one lives, the more accustomed we become to having them around, and we are lulled into a fantasy of immortality.

Our grief is justified, and no one can provide a satisfying reason why those we care for are snatched from our midst before their time.

But there are partial answers, and there are heroic figures who die young, who do so with such heroism and acceptance that they can provide models for others who grieve. Not to remove the grief, but to soften it, and hasten the healing process that must take place after loss.

The famous athlete Arthur Ashe, world tennis champion and respected scholar of African American history, provided just such words of comfort in his memoirs. He writes, in part:

"Since the news that I have AIDS was made public, quite often people who mean well will inquire of me whether I ever ask myself, in the face of my many diseases, 'Why me?' I never do. If I ask 'Why me?' as I am assaulted by heart disease and AIDS, I must also ask 'Why me?' about my blessings, and question my right to enjoy them. The morning after I won Wimbledon in 1975, I should have asked, 'Why me?', and doubted that I deserved the victory. If I don't ask 'Why me? after my victories, I cannot ask 'Why me?' after my setbacks and tragedies."

-Rabbi Dov Peretz Elkins

The Process of Mourning

From the 17th of Tammuz until the ninth of Av is a period of three weeks of mourning for the destruction of the Temple. The mourning gradually increases in intensity, culminating in a day of fasting and remembrance.

When someone close to us dies, the process is reversed. Gradually the intensity of mourning decreases, from the week of shiva to sheloshim – the 30 days following death – to the year of saying Kaddish, the mourning prayer.

Why does the first process grow and the second diminish? Because, teaches Rabbi J.B. Soloveitchik, each is designed to connect the mourner to the Jewish people. The individual mourner must be brought back to people out of private grief. And the worshiper approaching Tisha b'Av must be induced to take part in the collective memory of the Jewish people. Each needs to join something larger than himself, one through community, the other through history.

When private tragedy strikes, we need the warmth of others. When there is a collective tragedy, the calamities of others must become ours as well. Mourning is a letting go and a rejoining. Miguel De Unamuno wrote, "The great sanctity of a Temple is that it is where men go to weep together." Our tradition teaches us that no one need grieve alone.

-Rabbi David Wolpe

God Has Given, God Has Taken – May the Name of God Be Blessed

Adonai natan, v'Adonai lakach.
God has given, God has taken.
Yehi shem Adonai mevorach.
May the name of God be blessed.

At dozens and dozens of funerals, I have led friends, congregants and family through the recitation of these words. But eight weeks ago, as I said them at my mother's funeral,the experience was unprecedented for me. I've been in this movie before, I thought, but I was always playing a different part. Even at the funerals of my grandparents, and of friends, my role was always to "take care" of the mourners who were "closer in" to the circle of grief than I was. And here I was, at the innermost circle.

I would like to tell you what it's like to be at that innermost circle – from a Jewish perspective. What it was like for me to endure this tragedy through a Jewish lens. I've actually planned for a long time, for several years, to give a sermon like this. I just didn't think it was going to be about me. Now, I harbor no illusion that the way I responded to my grief is exactly the way that others might respond to theirs. Grief is very individual, and the 400 people or so in this synagogue right now have at least 400 different kinds of relationships to Jewish tradition. The choices I made may not be entirely the choices you would make. But I found the rituals of Jewish tradition to be extraordinarily powerful, helpful and comforting. And to tell you about my experiences, and the roles that Jewish teachings and traditions played for me over these last several weeks, is a way for me to wrest some blessing even from the midst of sorrow. And unfortunately, almost all of us will face some kind of grief and mourning in the future. So the perspective I can provide may be, for some, a practical guide to issues that *you* may face, as *you* seek to discern the role that Jewish tradition will play in *your* life.

Tuesday morning: I was in my office downstairs when I got the call with the news. The only way that I know how I reacted was that about five minutes later, Rachelle, our pre-school director, came knocking at my door because she was concerned that there must be a crying infant or toddler there. How thankful I am for a religious and cultural tradition that completely abandons the figment of the "stiff upper lip," that wishes to affirm emotions rather than trying to control or stifle them. Very sensibly, the Talmud tells us: *al tenachamenu be-sha'ah she-meito mutal lefanav* (Avot 4:18) – Don't even bother trying to comfort your friend, when his deceased relative is still lying unburied. It won't work, and it will just add insult to injury. And it goes even further. For those in the state of *aninut*, that stage of absolutely brutal, painful sorrow amidst the shock of the death, not only are you not supposed to be comforted; you're not supposed to do any of the *mitzvot.* You're not supposed to take *any* affirmative steps to fulfill *any* positive precept of Jewish tradition, with the exception of ensuring prompt burial for your loved one. Now obviously, this will affect people differently depending on how many mitzvot they are doing on a daily basis. For me, prayer normally punctuates my day – and saying blessings before and after I eat is basically automatic for me. But after hearing the news of the loss, Jewish tradition asks me not to pray, not to say blessings before and after meals, not to give *tzedakah* – essentially not to do any religious act until I have had a chance to get the minimal emotional closure that burial can provide.

Why? Some say it's so I can better focus on the task at hand. And some say I shouldn't say blessings at this stage because blessing seems so truly absent from my life. And like a treasured friend, like a good listener, Judaism doesn't want to drag me away from my emotional state. Judaism wants to *affirm* the emotional state where I currently am. No blessings; no words of comfort. I usually thrive on both; but at that moment, I had no patience for either.

Tuesday night: My family has finally arrived at my parents' home in Maryland. We are preparing for the funeral tomorrow morning. And my first true moment of comfort comes – surprisingly enough – while I am on the phone with my parents' rabbi. When he says to me: "I wanted to let you know that the *Hevra Kadisha* finished the *taharah* for your mother." So what does this mean? It means: the group of volunteers who form the *Hevra Kadisha* – the synagogue funeral and burial committee – have just completed the ritual washing of her body and putting her burial shrouds on her. And for the first time that day, I feel a calm wash over me. It was not paid functionaries who attended to the final earthly needs of my mother's body. It was volunteers – volunteers from her synagogue – a squad of about four women came to the funeral home. (For modesty's sake, women wash women, men wash men.) They recited some prayers as they prepared her for burial as an act of communal love and dedication. Perhaps they knew my mother from synagogue life; perhaps not. I can't imagine how difficult psychologically that volunteer opportunity is, how brave these people are, to donate their weeknights, on just a few hours' notice, to attend to the needs of the dead. I should add that for a period of time in my childhood, my mother was one of these brave women on the *Hevra Kadisha*. Me, I've never done it – for a variety of reasons and excuses, but frankly the most significant of which is – I'm scared. But I found myself full of gratitude. The *Hevra Kadisha* reminds me of an earlier time, when death was truly seen as a natural part of life, an organic process that was not sterile or hidden away. No wonder the literal translation of *Hevra Kadisha* is "society of holiness."

Wednesday morning: I have known for a long time that when the time came for me to do the ritual of *k'riah*, tearing an article of clothing immediately before the funeral, I knew that a symbolic black ribbon was not going to be sufficient for me. If my ancestors, with just two or three sets of clothing, actually tore their clothing, then surely I can find a shirt in the back of my closet that I'm never going to wear again. Tradition says that upon the conclusion of 30 days, I am allowed to mend the gash that I make in my shirt. But just a basting, not a professional mend, to mirror how loss works. Eventually the hole in our hearts starts to close up, but never perfectly, and it is never the same as it was before. Seems only theoretical to me. Not only do I have no plans to mend the shirt, but I could not imagine that gaping hole in my heart ever healing. At that moment I wonder if I will be feeling this much pain forever.

Walking into the chapel where the funeral will take place, I see the casket – the proverbial "plain pine box" that puts my mother in continuity with dozens of generations of ancestors, that reminds us that in death, all distinctions of rich and poor, high or low status, is rendered strictly irrelevant. And I realize that at this moment of discontinuity I treasure any link between the generations, any reminder that my mother is actually a part of a tradition much greater than herself, which began long before her birth and that – God willing – will continue long after her death. Some aspects of the funeral service focus on her distinctive personality, values, relationships and achievements, while other aspects of the funeral put her in the context of all of Jewish tradition. And it's that combination that provides the comfort.

Wednesday afternoon: We stand at the cemetery, shoveling earth into the grave. My older daughters solemnly share in this task. Later on, some people would approach us at shiva and tell us how they were a bit surprised that we had brought our children to the funeral and burial – all our daughters, age 7, age 4, and age 1-1/2. Weren't we concerned that it would be disturbing to them? In truth, Naomi and I never actually discussed it. It was just an automatic assumption, a value we knew we shared – of course we would bring them. And yes, it might be difficult for them – but not appreciably more difficult than suddenly losing their grandmother, and quite possibly it would be a source of comfort to them, and without a doubt they would be a source of comfort to us. And this is why we brought them also to the funeral of my grandfather, and to shiva for both of my grandparents who died this past year. It is not our job to shield our children from all the pain of the world, but rather to help them to face that pain from which we can't shield them with confidence and strength. Throughout their lives, my children will always know that their bond with their Savta, their grandmother, included participating in the task of *hesed shel emet* – assisting in someone's burial, that truest act of loving-kindness because it's the one thing that can never be reciprocated.

Later on Wednesday afternoon: I have sometimes thought that a casual visitor to our pre-school, listening to the Jewish songs we teach the kids, songs about challah and wine, and Shabbat dinner, and apples dipped in honey, and latkes sizzling in the pan, would conclude that Judaism really is all about food. I think you could have come to a similar conclusion if you looked at my parents' home on the first afternoon of shiva. When you want so much to help and comfort someone, and you know that there's almost nothing you can say that will really be a source of comfort, it's much easier to express that love and concern through food. Now let me tell you – my parents for their entire lives have been givers, not takers. And that's the way my brother and I were raised. Far better to give than to receive – in fact, receiving is always a little awkward. The thought of all this food – gifts of food – entering my parents' home was uncomfortable. But perhaps it was our first lesson that – at a time of need – we had better learn how to stop giving for a while, and just to sit, and receive – to let other people do things for us.

I've told so many people who are grieving that they shouldn't be surprised if they find the acts of mourning and grieving to be absolutely exhausting and draining, much more so than their normal work and their normal routine. No wonder it's called *sitting* shiva. I get up to make myself a sandwich, and one of my mom's friends tells me – "you – sit. I'll get your food. What do you want?" And I know at that moment that we are playing roles in a cosmic drama – that just as much as I need her to provide for my needs, she has a deep need herself to take care of me.

All the food accumulates in the kitchen, meticulously labeled with the names of who provided it, what the ingredients are, in some cases what *kashrut* standards were used in preparing it. Except for one gift bag containing three delicious home-grown tomatoes, evidently from someone's garden, that seems to have no name on it. Until my sister-in-law notices that there is actually a tiny little gift card attached to the bag. She opens it and reads it. It says: "Mazal Tov! Enjoy living in your new home. Fondly, Ella and Stan." (The names have been changed to protect the innocent!) We simply erupt in uproarious laughter. An even better gift than the tomatoes is the chance to laugh for the first time in days. I knew a gift can sometimes be a faux pas, but I didn't realize that a faux pas could actually be a gift.

Monday morning: Someone from this community visits me for shiva, now relocated to Hoboken, and gives me a hug and says, "There's never anything good to say." And he's right. I've taught before that the comfort at a time of bereavement comes not primarily from people's words, but from the mere fact of their presence. And now I really know how true that is. One of my friends and colleagues reminded me that in the

Sefardic tradition, what you're supposed to say to someone who is bereaved is *tenuchamu min ha-shamayim*, which means "may you be comforted from heaven," as if to say: authentic comfort is unlikely to come from anywhere else. The Biblical precursor to the observance of shiva is found in the book of Job, where Job's three friends visit him as he mourns for his losses, and join with him in sitting on the floor and crying with him for seven days. And they don't actually say anything to him – they are comforting just with their presence. Then after seven days one of them starts to speak. Let's just say that they were doing a better job when they stayed silent. And I noticed for myself – though of course some may perceive this differently – was not the content of what people said to me that provided the comfort, but rather the fact that you were there saying it. And it was not the content of the cards and notes, but the *fact* that you took the time and energy to send them. With one exception: when people had either known my mother, or read my eulogy and commented specifically about my mother's life, *that* was extraordinary. That, I lived for. But in general, when it comes to helping someone at a time of grief, perhaps the best advice is counter-intuitive. Don't just say something – stand there.

Shiva is like a trust-fall game, one of those group-building games you play at summer camp, where you are supposed to close your eyes and lean back into nothingness, just trusting that the other people in the group will catch you. And I was caught. I was caught *so* well, by this community and my parents' community, that by this point during shiva, I was starting to say, when people asked me about my week, that I had experienced the most terrible thing, but it was followed by a succession of only wonderful things. This is a credit to some extraordinary communities in Hoboken and in Maryland. But it is also a credit, frankly, to my parents: to the lives they have led, the attachments they have forged, the love and devotion they have shown to others, throughout their lives that was now being reciprocated. I would love to say that the outpouring of love and support that my father is currently receiving from his community is a birthright to which any Jew in a similar need is entitled. But it is not. The full extent of the communal response to my father's needs is – frankly – a right due to someone who has lived an unselfish life, devoted to the needs of the community. It's the bank of social capital: the more you deposit, the more you can withdraw. Every so often you should check your balance.

Wednesday, September 20: It's 1:35 p.m.; I'm on the 2nd floor of the Newport Tower in Jersey City, waiting outside a locked door. Exactly at 1:36 p.m. and 30 seconds, someone comes to unlock the door. Within the next three-and-a-half minutes, the unpainted and unfinished room behind the door is suddenly full of men who have seemingly come out of nowhere – but actually have come from the various office buildings on Washington Boulevard. And promptly at 1:40 p.m., we begin the daily *mincha* – afternoon service – with some communal chanting in Hebrew, some silent prayer, some individual chanting, and we conclude with the Mourner's Kaddish, which I lead together with the other mourners present. By 1:50 p.m., the brief service has concluded. By 1:51 p.m., with the room empty and the door locked, you could not possibly have believed that that room had been used as a makeshift synagogue. There are various places I have gone over these weeks to gather with a minyan – with a quorum of 10 adult Jews – for daily prayer services, morning, afternoon, and evening, and for me to be one of the leaders of the Mourner's Kaddish. Some of those places are familiar and comfortable, like here in this sanctuary. Some of those places remain completely foreign to me, no matter how many times I go there, like the Hasidic synagogue in Union City. And some are simply unlikely or unusual, like the minyan in the Newport Tower.

A couple of weeks after my mother died, Naomi and I and our kids took a previously scheduled trip to the Boston area. And in advance, I had scouted out synagogues in proximity to each place we were visiting, so I could pray and say Kaddish with a minyan each morning, afternoon and evening. The image in my mind – though of course it is an imperfect analogy for a host of reasons – was that of a dialysis patient on vacation, who has to seek out other places to receive life-sustaining treatments, even away from home. When I gathered with a minyan – and in Boston, it was always a minyan of complete strangers – I felt them holding my hand, sustaining me, and leading me back towards wholeness.

And just like the food at the shiva house, saying Kaddish is another kind of training for the mourner to be willing to take, not merely to give. Almost every daily minyan I go to is somewhat precarious. Assembling 10 people is not the easiest task. And I have no illusions that being at a prayer service is exactly where all those people want to be at that very moment. Daily *minyanim* are sustained by people pledging *responsibility* – people who are giving the free-will gift of their presence. And I am conscious that I am benefiting from their generosity.

I think about how the Kaddish prayer is thousands of years old, but there was no such thing as the Mourner's Kaddish until approximately the era of the Crusades. The Mourner's Kaddish may not mention death, but speaking historically, it grew out of one of the most famous Jewish ghost stories. The *Or Zarua*, a text from Central Europe in the 1100s, is the first to tell the story – of how the esteemed Rabbi Akiva once saw a ghost, a disembodied soul, engaged in hard labor. The dead man tells Rabbi Akiva that he is doomed to hard labor forever, but he would be freed from punishment immediately if his son were to stand before the congregation and say *Yitgadal ve-yitkadash shemeih rabbah* – "Let God's holy name be magnified and sanctified," and the congregation would respond: *"yehei shmeih rabbah mevarach."* – "May God's great name be praised." But the man laments: who would teach my son? I have no friends in the world!" Rabbi Akiva then commits himself to finding this man's son and teaching him enough Hebrew so he can lead the community in prayer. Though the son is not a particularly motivated student, eventually he learns to say the words *"yitgadal ve-yitkadash shemeih rabbah,"* and the community responds with the words, *"yehei shmeih rabba mevarach,"* may God's great name be praised.

The next night, Rabbi Akiva has a dream in which the deceased man thanks him profusely, because this has indeed liberated him from his torments. And as the story spread, so did the practice of children of deceased parents leading the

Kaddish. It is meritorious for children of deceased parents to be the ones to invite the entire community to praise God's name. Because that's what the Kaddish really is – it's a delivery system for Divine praise. It's an invitation for the community to praise God's name.

So is this why I am saying the Kaddish three times (almost) every day, for almost a year? Is it to liberate my mother's soul from its hard labor? Actually, my picture of the afterlife looks somewhat different from this. Plus, try as I may, I can't believe there are any sins that my mom is being punished for. The greatest gift that saying Kaddish gives to me is the gift of regularity, of a structure in which to remember her, every day, in the presence of a community. But I am also intrigued by this idea; that the way that I best honor my mother's memory is by inviting people to praise God, to increase the quotient of God-praise in the world. And so, for several months, those who have suffered losses are asked to wander the world as freelance itinerant God-praise-inviters. The Kaddish is said only with a minyan, since a minyan is the minimum number of people who can truly speak for the Jewish people. Every time you assemble a minyan, you have reached a quorum. Every minyan is really a meeting of the Jewish people in conference assembled. And so, as the meeting comes to order, I make a motion: *yitgadal ve-yitkadash shemeih rabbah.* On behalf of the Jewish people in their entirety, let us praise God. In memory of my mother. And so, in communities that are so diverse geographically and ideologically, I assist in spreading the God-praise. Because henceforth, there's really only one kind of gift I can give to my mother anymore that really matters. I can live my life in such a way that it motivates praise of God. I can strive to make the world better, in her name.

I notice just how often it is that I show up at a minyan, somewhere, and I realize that there are only ten Jewish adults there. If I hadn't shown up, they wouldn't have had a minyan. And gradually, it happens more and more that I meet other people whose losses are more recent than mine. Someone who just completed the shiva mourning period. Someone who is earlier on the emotional arc of grief than I am. I look at them, and I remember what it was like back when I was there. I hadn't noticed, but I have come a long way in a short time. They look at me as a signpost further on the way towards wholeness. And we each benefit from each other's presence. And gradually, it happens more and more that I officiate at funerals, and visit people during shiva, and I may act exactly the same as before, but in some intangible way, the interaction is different. Just as during shiva, I found myself yearning to spend the most time with my friends who had lost parents themselves.

I never realized that so much of Jewish grieving and mourning is about learning how to take, and learning how to give again. When we give, obviously we are emulating God. But perhaps we are also emulating God when we take. Because I have to hope and pray that it is at least as painful and agonizing for God to learn how to take as it is for us.

> *Adonai natan v'Adonai lakah.*
> God has given, God has taken.
> *Yehi shem Adonai mevorach.*
> *Yehei shmeih rabba mevarach.*
> Praised be God's name.

-Rabbi Robert Scheinberg

When Someone Grieves

What do you say to someone who is grieving? ("Other than that, Mrs. Lincoln, how did you like the play?" probably tops the list of the kinds of conversation starters that should be avoided.) And actually, there are a lot of ways we can go wrong here – saying something that isn't appreciated by one who hurts. Even when we are trying to comfort.

But chances are, we have been, or will be, put in the position of trying to comfort someone who is experiencing a painful loss. That is an important role we all play from time to time. So, what do you say to someone who is grieving?

I often remember a story told by Joseph Bayly when I struggle to say the "right thing" to someone who is hurting. Mr. Bayly lost three children to death over the course of several years. He wrote a book called *View from a Hearse*, in which he talks about his grief. He says this about comforting those who grieve:

"I was sitting, torn by grief. Someone came and talked to me of God's dealings, of why it happened, of hope beyond the grave. He said things I knew were true. I was unmoved, except to wish he would go away. He finally did. Someone else came and sat beside me. He didn't talk. He didn't ask leading questions. He just sat with me for an hour or more, listened when I said something, answered briefly, prayed simply, left. I was moved. I was comforted. I hated to see him go."

I have found Joseph Bayly's experience to be excruciatingly typical. Both men wanted to help. Both men cared. But only one truly comforted. The difference was that one tried to make him feel better, while the other just let him feel. One tried to say the right things. The other listened. One told him it would be all right. The other shared his pain.

When put in the difficult position of comforting someone in emotional pain, sometimes what needs to be said can be said best with a soft touch or a listening ear. No words. And though at times the quieter approach has felt inadequate to me, I have come to realize that it can make a bigger difference than I may ever know.

-Steve Goodier

Finding the Right Words

Have you ever noticed how hard it can be to find the right words? It was once said that Al Smith, former governor of New York, was making his first inspection of Sing Sing prison. The warden asked him if he might say a few words to the prisoners.

The governor began, "My fellow citizens." But he suddenly felt confused about whether the inmates may have forfeited their citizenship. So he took a second stab at it: "My fellow convicts." There was a roar of laughter and now he became flustered. He gallantly tried a third time: "Well, anyhow, I'm glad to see so many of you here." There is no record of what he said after that. I have frequently struggled to find the right words. And there are times I am certain the right words do not even exist. Like when I'm trying to say something hopeful or comforting in a particularly frightening situation.

More than once I have been called to a hospital emergency room or to be with a family surrounding the bed of a dying relative. And more than once I've been at a loss for words. What is the right thing to say at a time like that? What can I say that doesn't sound hollow or trite or like I'm just not in touch with the feelings of others who are hurting?

A lot of us really don't know what to say at these times. And too often the professionals who work daily with people on the ragged edge of hope have become so desensitized they have lost any ability to comfort.

A wise obstetrician at a university teaching hospital once made a comment about comforting those who suffer. Someone asked the doctor what advice he offered his students, future doctors and nurses, when caring for mothers who gave birth to stillborn infants.

The doctor paused for a moment in thought. Then he said this: "I tell them that they need two eyes. One eye is not enough; they need two eyes. With one eye they have to check the I.V. And with the other eye they have to weep. That's what I tell them," he said. "I tell them that they need two eyes."

That may be some of the wisest advice I've ever heard. We may not always need to figure out what to say; we really only need two eyes. In Emily Dickinson's words, "Saying nothing sometimes says the most." And this from a poet whose life was all about finding exactly the right words.

I agree with the doctor – empathy goes a long way. And somehow finding the ability to feel, even for a few moments, what another is feeling may speak more loudly than the best words I can choose. It speaks to the fact that I care; I understand. It says that I am willing to share their pain so they do not feel so alone. It says I want to be fully present with them and to walk alongside of them, difficult as it may be. My presence is something they can draw real strength and hope from.

Come to think of it, maybe Dickinson did find the right words: saying nothing ... sometimes says the most. And saying nothing at all may be just the right thing to say.

-Steve Goodier

On Grief

We are allowed to be deeply into basketball, or Buddhism, or Star Trek, or jazz, but we are not allowed to be deeply sad. Grief is a thing that we are encouraged to "let go of," to "move on from," and we are told specifically how this should be done. Countless well-intentioned friends, distant family members, hospital workers, and strangers I met at parties recited the famous five stages of grief to me: denial, anger, bargaining, depression, and acceptance. I was alarmed by how many people knew them, how deeply this single definition of the grieving process had permeated our cultural consciousness. Not only was I supposed to feel these five things, I was meant to feel them in that order and for a prescribed amount of time.

We like to say how things are, perhaps because we hope that's how they might actually be. We attempt to name, identify, and define the most mysterious of matters: sex, love, marriage, monogamy, infidelity, death, loss, grief. We want these things to have an order, an internal logic, and we also want them to be connected to one another. We want it to be true that if we cheat on our spouse, it means we no longer want to be married to him or her. We want it to be true that if someone we love dies, we simply have to pass through a series of phases, like an emotional obstacle course from which we will emerge happy and content, unharmed and unchanged.

After my mother died, everyone I knew wanted to tell me either about the worst breakup they'd had or all the people they'd known who'd died. I listened to a long, traumatic story about a girlfriend who suddenly moved to Ohio, and to stories of grandfathers and old friends and people who lived down the block who were no longer among us. Rarely was this helpful.

Occasionally I came across people who'd had the experience of losing someone whose death made them think, *I cannot continue to live.* I recognized these people: their postures, where they rested their eyes as they spoke, the expressions they let onto their faces and the ones they kept off. These people consoled me beyond measure. I felt profoundly connected to them, as if we were a tribe.

-Cheryl Strayed

Together – We Can Stand Anything

Maybe some of you have seen California's magnificent Sequoias. Did you know that these trees, some of which are as tall as a skyscraper, have roots practically at surface level? A lone sequoia's roots are so shallow that it can hardly stand up to a strong breeze. So how do they grow so tall? They spring up in groves, and their roots intertwine. In other words, they hold each other up–they give each other the strength necessary to withstand the angriest winds. And it is the same with us. Alone we can kvetch and *hok me a tcheinook* ... alone we will know pain. But when we are together ... we can stand anything.

-*Rabbi Dannel I. Schwartz*

The Metaphysics of Mourning

How can we tell where one person ends and another begins? The material finitude of our bodies is evident, but the borders of the soul are less definite. We merge as we learn from one another, live together and accrue common experiences, take on each other's projects, and enter into shared fates. Love blurs the boundaries between one soul and another. In fact, love might be defined as that very erosion, absorption, commingling.

When the tenuous coupling of a person's body and soul is undone by death, the bond of body and soul within each person who has been close to the *met/metah* is also weakened. The breath of God within all who were bound up with that person wishes, as it were, to leave the bodies of its temporary residence and to flee to the one great Source. And so it is that a survivor must mourn, to heal and repair the bond between his or her own body and soul – literally, in some measure, to stay alive.

Anthropologist Victor Turner speaks of liminality, of a time when everything is changing, when a person is especially vulnerable, almost as though his or her skin were missing. At such a time, Turner says, the community comes together, the tradition steps in, and together we walk the person through the tunnel of liminality to a new place in a world reconnected.

Mourning is perhaps the ultimate liminal, or disconnected, state. Outside us, the web of life has been torn. Within us, body and soul may have been severed almost instantaneously for the loved one who died, the reweaving of body and soul in the survivors – the agenda of mourning – happens in stages over weeks, months, years, and generations. No wonder, then, that the reuniting of the bodies and souls of all people for the great messianic resurrection is imagined to require millennia of preparation.

-Rabbi Margaret Holub

A Letter to My Niece About Death

For Talia:

It's going to be difficult for all of us to be at the memorial service. But it is a mitzvah to dedicate a place that holds the memory of Nana. For me, I don't believe that *she* is there. I think her spirit is everywhere now, like God's, but at the cemetery we make a special place out of respect for her and then sometimes visit there, and meditate, think about things and invite her memory to be there again with us.

Nana's body was buried carefully and lovingly in that place. She didn't need it anymore. It's like the caterpillar that becomes a butterfly. Imagine that the caterpillar is like the body and the butterfly is Nana's spirit or soul. The caterpillar goes through some big changes. It goes into a cocoon, sheds it skin, comes out a butterfly and flies away. So, what happened to the caterpillar? Did it die? It must certainly think it's dying for good when it goes into that dark cocoon. And yet it changed into something else – a butterfly. I guess it sort of "died into a butterfly."

Even so, if I were that caterpillar's buddy, I still might miss my friend very much.

I don't think that anything ever dies, really dies. I think things, people, animals, insects ... everything, just changes the way it looks and stuff, but their soul and spirit (and everyone has these) is forever and ever. I think that even trees have spirits. Do you?

How this happens is a great mystery. In a movie I once saw, the old actor George Burns was playing God and a kid asked him why there were bad things in the world, like criminals and sickness. George Burns answered that he tried to make an up without a down, an in without an out, light without darkness, good without bad, life without death, but couldn't do it. It's even hard to imagine, isn't it?

So, it's all a mystery.

Mysteries keep life very interesting and challenging (But then maybe God couldn't make an "easy" without a "hard" either). One of the best things is that when everything isn't all figured out for us, and there are mysteries, then we get to try to figure things out for ourselves, and that can be fun. It's like working on a big puzzle. The *best* puzzle. Everyone has their own idea about what's the best way to put the puzzle together. That's why there are lots of different philosophies and different religions (people who think that their beliefs and behaviors will bring them closer to understanding the puzzle, or at least help them to live better with The Mystery).

Living with a mystery isn't easy.

I wish people didn't die. Even little changes are hard. A big change like someone being gone that we liked very much and who liked us a lot is the pits. But nobody asked us, and I don't like thinking about how scary that is. But I do know that I can't even make grass grow and God can make a whole elephant. If God can make a forest from a seed, then maybe God knows more about this situation than I do and so maybe I ought to trust a little more. Maybe things are exactly the way they are supposed to be. After all, left up to me, I'd probably try to save the caterpillar and it would never get to be a butterfly.

I expect things will continue to grow and change in ways that I sometimes won't like at all and may never understand. When something changes too fast for me, like when a terrible thing happens, then I find that talking with God and to people I love helps a lot. It doesn't make the person be alive again, but I feel better, stronger and in good company. Of course I like to just be left alone and miserable (well I don't like it, but it seems like the right thing to do at the time).

As I get even older I think I can accept living with The Mystery better. I don't know why.

I guess that's just another mystery.

Love, Aunty Sandy

-Sandra Shaw Friedman

A Grand Send-Off

At Bubbe Jenny's funeral, I knew in my heart that she was watching us. She always loved people and would have delighted in seeing so many of us gathered together. In my eulogy, I spoke about her long life and her impact on the people who had known her. I then said to those gathered, "We all have memories of Bubbe Jenny, a picture in our mind of her speaking, laughing, telling a story: Take a moment and let a memory or an image of her come to mind." I paused, then continued, "Our Jewish tradition suggests that right now she may be somewhere in an afterlife, a realm we do not know very much about; but let us hold that picture or memory of her in our minds, and let us all send her love as she commences her journey in the afterlife." I then stopped speaking and we spent a moment in silence – it was very powerful. I had the sense we were giving Bubbe Jenny a grand send-off to the other world.

-*Jewish Pastoral Care* 2nd Ed., p. 410

♦♦♦

Comfort, oh comfort my people, says your God.

-*Isaiah* 40:1

The Power of Tears

It happened once that a very sad woman went to visit Rabbi Aryeh Levin, and asked if she could sit with him a while to cry her heart out.

You can sit, of course, said Rabbi Aryeh. But crying – you have to cry before the Blessed Holy One, not to me. God hears the sound of crying, and listens to the anguish of His children.

The woman sat across from him, and cried and cried and cried. She told him all the troubles her husband was having. He was mortally ill.

Don't cry, said the rabbi. God will have pity and heal him.

Several days later he heard that her husband had died. Rabbi Aryeh went to comfort her, and found her crying bitterly. Rabbi Aryeh comforted her and encouraged her with words that entered her heart.

I will be comforted, she said to him, as long as you can tell me what happened to the torrent of my tears, tears with which I moistened the Book of Psalms in my hand, all the days that I cried before the Blessed Holy One during the time my late husband was ill.

Rabbi Aryeh replied: "In 120 years from now, when you stand before the heavenly court, you will find out how many harsh decrees on our people were canceled due to the pure tears that poured from your eyes. No tears are lost. The Blessed Holy One counts every tear and collects them in His precious storehouse of tears."

Again the woman burst out in tears, but this time in tears of joy.

After some time the widow returned to Rabbi Aryeh's home and said: "Rabbi, tell me again the same beautiful words. What was the fate of my many tears?"

-Unknown

Driving Sorrow Out of Your Life

There is an old Chinese tale about the woman whose only son died. In her grief she went to the holy man and asked, "What prayers, what magical incantations do you have to bring my son back to life?" Instead of sending her away, he said, "Fetch me a mustard seed from a home that has never known sorrow. We will use it to drive the sorrow out of your life."

The woman set off at once in search of the magical mustard seed. She came first to a splendid mansion, knocked at the door, and said, "I am looking for a home that has never known sorrow. Is this such a place?" They told her, "You've certainly come to the wrong house" and began describing all the tragic things that had recently befallen them. The woman said to herself, "Who is better able to help these poor unfortunate people than I, who have had misfortune of my own?"

She stayed to comfort them for a while, then went on in her search for a home that had never known sorrow. But wherever she turned, in hovels and in palaces, she found one tale after another of sadness or misfortune.

Ultimately, she became so involved in ministering to other

people's grief, that she forgot about her quest for the magical mustard seed, never realizing that it had in fact already driven the sorrow out of her life.

-Rabbi Steven Carr Reuben

Helping the Living

This is the story of a miracle.

It was a miracle witnessed by a recording clerk in a cemetery. Every week, for several years, this mild little man had received a letter from a woman he did not know, enclosing a money order and directing him to put fresh flowers on the grave of her son. Then one day he met her face to face. A car drove up to the cemetery gates and a chauffeur hastened into the tiny administration building to speak to the birdlike little clerk whose hands fluttered over the papers on his desk.

"The lady outside is too ill to walk," he explained. "Would you mind coming with me?"

Waiting in the car was a frail elderly woman with a face whose imperious eyes could not hide some deep, long-lasting hurt. In her arms was a great heap of flowers.

"I am Mrs. Adams," she explained. "Every week for years I have been sending you a five-dollar money order."

"For the flowers!" the clerk exclaimed.

"Yes – to be laid on the grave of my son."

"I have never failed to attend to it," chirped the little man.

"I came here today," Mrs. Adams confided softly, "because the doctors have let me know I have only a few weeks left. But before I die I wanted to drive here for one last look and place the flowers myself."

The little clerk blinked up at her irresolutely. Then, with a wry smile, he made up his mind and spoke.

"You know, ma'am, I was always sorry you kept sending the money for the flowers."

"Sorry?"

"Yes – because the flowers last such a little while! And nobody ever could see them or smell them. It was a shame."

"Do you realize what you are saying?"

"Oh, please don't be angry. I belong to a visiting society. State hospitals. Insane asylums. People in places like that dearly love flowers, and they can see them and can smell them. Lady, there's living people in places like that. But there isn't anybody in that grave. Not really."

The woman did not answer, but sat for a brief while, silently repeating a prayer. When she left, without a word, the little clerk feared that his impulsive frankness might have overcome her, might even have hastened her end.

But some months later he was astonished to have another visit; doubly astonished, in fact, because there was no chauffeur this time; the woman sat at the wheel, driving her car alone.

"I take the flowers to the people myself," she confided with a friendly smile. "You were right; it does make them happy. And it makes me happy. The doctors don't know what is making me well – but I do! I have something to live for now!"

She had discovered what most of us know and forget – in helping others, she had miraculously helped herself. It is still true that our chief need in life is somebody who shall make us do what we can. Nothing makes us so strong as a cry for help.

-Fulton Oursler

The Wisdom of Accepting the Inevitable

Much of our happiness and our misery spring entirely from our attitude toward events. It depends on how you look at a thing – how you change it, or else how you accept it. There's no use fighting the inevitable. The only way to argue with a cold wind is to put on your overcoat. And then there's that famous prayer: "God grant me the courage to change the things I can change, and the serenity to accept the things I cannot change, and the wisdom to know the difference."

Like the soldier who lost his arm. Or did he?

This soldier was wounded in one of the early battles of the Second World War. On the operating table in a field hospital he opened his eyes and saw a doctor bending over him.

"It's all right, kid," the surgeon was saying, "you're going to get well. But I'm afraid you've lost your arm."

The soldier grinned, and in a faint voice replied: "I didn't lose my arm – I gave it."

In great matters and small, what happens to us is not nearly so important as our attitude toward it. The future of that maimed soldier was full of hope because of his positive point of view. He did not yield to despair. Every misfortune in life is an opportunity for advancement in spiritual strength for which we should be truly grateful. It all depends on how we meet God's challenge to us.

-Fulton Oursler

Life Is Not Lost If We Can Touch The Tears – A Yizkor Reflection

The story of Moshe's life begins with a cry, in the basket in the bulrush, and it also ends with a cry.

After Moshe's death, the rabbis relate that not only did the children of Israel cry, but his disciple, Joshua, unable to find his teacher and realizing that he was gone forever, began to cry. Then the heavens cried and the earth cried.

Finally, having taken Moshe's soul away with a kiss, even God cried.

We are here today to recite the Yizkor prayers – to cry for those who are gone and to remember how much a part of them we are. We are here to say that yes, we took a risk when we decided to love. We opened ourselves to great happiness and thus to great pain. But it was worth it. We would not have missed a minute of it, not any of it. None of the fullness of life is lost as long as we can remember the laughter and touch the tears.

-Rabbi Steven Saltzman

Not What You Lose

Franklin Delano Roosevelt was once asked how he could be a successful president having been paralyzed by polio.

He replied: "It's not what you lose but what you have left and what you do with it."

-D.P.E.

Good Grief

We often hear people speak of birth as a miracle. Seldom do we hear of death spoken of in the same way. But if there is something miraculous about life coming into existence, certainly the same holds true for death. To watch an active person reduced into inorganic nothingness before our very eyes is also a miracle, albeit a terrible one.

But if death is the other side of the coin which we call life, then grief is the other side of love. Bereavement is love not wanting to let go. Each tear we shed is a midwife which helps bring us into a new world. We mourn our loss. Then we face a new day. We turn a new page. We start a new chapter. We begin our own new life.

We are all terminal. From the moment we are born, we are destined to die. Our happiness is bound up in our ability to accept death as a fact of life. Acceptance of our mortal end is not something which comes easily. Such growth takes work. None of us have time to lose in accepting this reality.

How do we die? Each death, like each life, is unique. Some deaths are noble. Some are petty. Some are loving. Some are angry. Most are a combination of these things. But just as our lives are, to a great extent, at our command, so too are our deaths. Although we cannot determine precisely the day and hour of our passing or its ultimate cause, we can often orchestrate how we want our last days to be. We can live until we die.

Death is not entirely tragic. Our loved ones can bask in the afterglow of something that was once wonderful and be grateful that they once shared something beautiful with us.

As a rabbi, you might expect me to tell you that everything in the Bible is true. But I would be lying if I told you I believe that. We are taught "the Lord gives and the Lord takes away." But, in truth, not everything is taken from us. Memory is ours as long as we live.

Every person is like a snowflake. Every person, like every snowflake is unique. Both people and snowflakes have intricate patterns which have never been replicated and never will. Yet both people and snowflakes melt away before our eyes. Each is frail. Each is, in its own way, something beautiful. Each is so very delicate and vulnerable. Each is precious beyond words.

◆◆◆

Literature is full of "famous last words" by celebrated individuals. (It is simply amazing how loquacious some of these people were considering the state they were in.) Nowadays, due to improvements in palliative care, it is highly unlikely that we will be conscious enough to have that kind of lucidity. In all likelihood we will be tethered to all kinds of devices which are intended to ease our passing. While these improvements will make our deaths more comfortable, it will be at the expense of mental clarity.

The time to express one's thoughts and wishes is now.

When my mother died I inherited her needlepoint tapestries. When I was a little boy I used to sit at her feet as she worked on them. Have you ever seen needle point from underneath? All I could see was chaos, strands of thread all over with no seeming purpose. As I grew, I was able to view her work from above. I came to appreciate the intricate patterns. What is more, I learned that the dark patterns were every bit as essential to the success of the work as the bright and gaily colored ones. Sometimes I think that life is like that. From our human perspective, we cannot see the whole picture. We have a limited view of reality. Nevertheless, we should not despair that there is an explanation, meaning and purpose.

The Welsh poet Dylan Thomas wrote a poem reflecting on the death of his father: "Do not go gentle into that good night/ Old age should burn and rage at close of day / Rage, rage against the dying of the light." But in the end all rage and anger will pass. We will enter a realm of peace where nothing can hurt us, ever.

We are the people of the book. Each of us is an author writing the book of his or her life. Authors dream of their work becoming a classic, but few ever do. Whether or not the book of our lives becomes a classic depends on us, but not only on us. To an even greater extent it depends on those who remain behind. For what is a classic but a work to which others make reference after it is finished? It is not for us to finish the task.

Franz Rosenzweig concluded his classic, "*The Star Of Redemption*" with these words "To walk humbly with thy God – the words are written over the gate, which leads out of the mysterious-miraculous light of the divine sanctuary in which no person can remain alive. Whither, then, do the wings of the gate open? Thou knowest it not? *Into Life.*"

-Rabbi Kenneth L. Cohen

♦♦♦

They who sow in tears, in rejoicing shall they reap;
Although he goes weeping, bearing the seed,
He shall surely come rejoicing, carrying his sheaves.

-Psalm 126

What of the Things That Die While We Are Still Alive?

We recite Yizkor for those who have died, but what of those things that die while we are still alive? Where is the Yizkor for lost relationships, for dreams and loves that have died, for dimly remembered childhoods and homes and hopes? We live lifetimes of loss, and do not know how to grieve.

For many people, faith begins in the assurance that we will not lose. Soon they discover that this faith is a chimera. There is no promise of painless life. We can never know why the world is so arranged that loss is woven into the fabric of living. Faith that promises ease is false and unworthy.

Deep faith does not promise that we will never lose, but that we can make the losses of life meaningful. Out of patterns of pain as well as joy and love, we create a moral work of art. At each moment, circumstance confronts us with the possibility of climbing the ladder of loss to reach higher than we were before.

This year, let us resolve to take all of life – its tragedies as well as its gladness – and use them to make life more beautiful, more purposeful, more sacred.

– Rabbi David Wolpe

♦♦♦

God gives strength to the weary,
　　Fresh vigor to the spent.
Youths may grow faint and exhausted,
　　The young may stumble and fall;
But those who hope in Ado'nai,
　　Their strength will be renewed
As eagles renew their plumes
　　They shall run and not grow weary,
March and not grow faint.

-Isaiah 40:31

Of Joy and Sorrow

Then a woman said: Speak to us of Joy and Sorrow. And he answered: Your joy is your sorrow unmasked. And the self-same well from which your laughter rises was often times filled with tears. And how else can it be? The deeper that sorrow carves into your being, the more joy you can contain. Is not the cup that holds your wine, the very cup that was burned in the potter's oven? And is not the lute that soothes your spirit, the very wood that was hollowed with knives? When you are joyous, look deep into your heart – And you shall find it is only that which has given you sorrow that is giving you joy. When you are sorrowful, look again into your heart and you will see that in truth you are weeping for that which has been your delight. Some of you say, "joy is greater than sorrow" – and others say, "nay, sorrow is the greater."

But I say unto you, they are inseparable. Together they come and when one sits alone with you at your board, remember that the other is asleep upon your bed.

-Khalil Gibran

Feeling the Sun From Both Sides

The bitter truth is that every love story has an unhappy ending, and the greater the love, the greater the unhappiness when it ends.

Whenever we love someone, we give a hostage to fortune.

Whenever we permit someone to become very dear to us, we become vulnerable to disappointment and heartbreak.

What, then, is our choice? Never permit ourselves to love anyone? Never permit anyone to matter to us? To deny ourselves the greatest of all God-given joys?

If loving is expensive, being unloved and unloving costs even more. I believe that even in our grief we can still agree that to love and be loved is to feel the sun from both sides.

-Rabbi Sidney Greenberg

Perspective

What about your life feels like a curse, like a dark cloud hanging over you? Is it something physical? Financial? The loss of a relationship or loved one? How might you change your perspective? Overcoming challenges can shape you into a stronger, more loving, more compassionate person. Those who focus only on the negative, tend to only see the curses in their lives. Focusing on the positive helps you learn from what is plaguing. It helps you to see the blessings even in the challenges you are facing in life. Sometimes you have to strain to see even a slightly positive aspect in your situation, but when you find it, grab on to it! Focus on it repeatedly, throughout the day, day after day, and in time, you may come to know the blessings hidden beneath it.

-Rabbi Philip Rice

Who Rekindles Your Light?

An insightful woman, who had lived through numerous dark nights and days, once taught me about getting through difficult times. "I appreciate your outlook on life," I commented to Mrs. Tucker. I was in my twenties and she was fifty years older. In the short time I knew her she became a significant teacher for me. I learned from her remarkable attitude and her unshakable strength of character, both of which undoubtedly buoyed her through treacherous waters.

"Well, I have been through a lot of tough times," she told me. "In fact, sometimes it was awfully hard for me and my husband. He couldn't always find work. Some days he would come home horribly depressed and say, 'Things are so bad I don't know if I can take it.' And I would say to him, 'Well, you know, things could be worse.' And once he said, 'I've heard that so many times I think I'm gonna die!' I was hurt ... but I just hated to see him so depressed. I didn't know what to say. Later he confessed that if I would have wept in despair, he wouldn't have been able to make it. He needed me during those times."

It occurs to me that HOW she responded to her husband's pain was probably not as important as the simple fact that she was there and cared. He knew he could always count on her to be a ray of light in his darkness and a strong hand to lift him when he stumbled or to soothe his hurts. He needed her ... and for similar reasons, she needed him, too.

Albert Schweitzer said so well, "Sometimes our light goes out but is blown into flame by another human being. Each of us owes deepest thanks to those who have rekindled this light." During those difficult times they rekindled one another's light.

Who rekindles your light? Who blows your light into flame when it threatens to flicker out? Sometimes this person is a relative, sometimes a teacher, or a pastor, or a close friend. I've learned that if I need the light of my spirit rekindled during a bleak time, there are a few special people who can do it.

I admire some people for their brilliance and I respect others for their strength. But I am indebted to those who can rekindle my spirit. I hope I can be such a person for others.

-Steve Goodier

When Suffering Visits

We are changed, sometimes in unexpected ways, by the problems of life.

One of Canada's most famous physicians was Dr. William Osler. Many stories are told of this beloved doctor, but one of the most revealing comes from World War I.

Friends recalled the day when Osler was working in one of Britain's military hospitals during the war. He was called out of the wards during his daily rounds to be given an important message; his own son had been killed on the fields of France.

Stunned by the news, he still came back to pick up his rounds. For a long period afterward he was noticeably different. And those who knew him best said that he changed as a physician that day. The cheerful note was gone from his voice and never again did friends hear the tune which he so often whistled as he went from ward to ward.

Though these things never returned, something eventually came to take their place. Everyone noticed a new compassion in his care of the soldiers who each day streamed in from the battlefield. Before, he had the professional concern of the physician, so important to the practice of medicine; now there was an added discernible note of personal compassion, like that of a father for his son.

Like most people who have experienced such losses, Osler must have spent considerable time in grief. But as he healed and integrated the loss into his life, it left him a different person.

Pain will do that. It changes us, often in unexpected ways. It can leave us angry and broken, or, as in the case of Osler, it can bring forth qualities such as compassion or tenderness. It is as if the physician channeled his pain into energy and love for others, caring for them as he would care for his own child.

Yes, the world is full of suffering. We can't avoid it no matter how hard we try. But it is also full of examples of people, like you and me, getting through it. Those who overcome great challenges will be changed, and often in unexpected ways. For our struggles enter our lives as unwelcome guests, but they bring valuable gifts. And once the pain subsides, the gifts remain.

These gifts are life's true treasures, bought at great price, but cannot be acquired in any other way.

-Steve Goodier

Love and Consolation

"And Isaac brought her (Rebeccah) into his mother Sarah's tent, and took Rebeccah, and she became his wife; and he loved her. And Isaac was comforted for his mother."

-Bereishith 24:67

The great medieval Bible commentator, Rabbi David Kimhi (known popularly as Radak), noted: "Although three years had passed between Sarah's death and Isaac's marriage to Rebeccah, yet he was mourning her (Sarah), and was comforted in that (Rebeccah) was good as his mother was."

It appears, then, that Isaac mourned his mother inconsolably for three years. But once Rebeccah entered his life, "he was comforted for his mother." Rebeccah had those qualities and virtues which characterized Sarah, and Isaac finally found consolation from the loss of his mother.

What is consolation?

Let us first state what consolation does not accomplish: it does not bring back the dead. It does not change reality. The beloved person has died and cannot be replaced.

Consolation does not deny reality. Rather, it attempts to cope with death by providing hope for the future. Death is a fact of human existence. It is distressing to lose a loved one. It is possible to sink into a deep depression when grieving. Consolation attempts to redirect mourning into a positive, future-oriented direction. Yes, a loved one has died; yes, the pain is real. No, the deceased loved one cannot be brought back to life.

Rabbi Joseph B. Soloveitchik, in a lecture in memory of his father, stated: "It seems to me as if my father were yet alive, although four years have come and gone since his death. It is in a qualitative sense that I experience his nearness and spirit tonight...Our sages have said...the righteous are exalted in death more than in life. If time be measured qualitatively, we may understand how their influence lingers on after their death and why the past is eternally bound with the present."

With the passage of time, the mourner comes to experience the presence of the deceased loved one with a "qualitative time-awareness." The focus is shifted from daily interactions that used to take place with the deceased. Instead, the mourner gains a deeper sense of the qualities and virtues of the deceased. With the passage of time, the mourning mellows into a calmer, wiser appreciation of the life of the one who has passed on. The bitter pain of mourning is softened. Consolation sets in.

Apparently, Isaac was so distraught at the passing of his mother that he had trouble developing this "qualitative time-awareness." Her death traumatized him, and he could not shake off his feelings of grief.

Let us remember the nature of the relationship between Sarah and her son, Isaac. She gave birth to him when she was already quite elderly. To her, Isaac was a miraculous gift from God. She must surely have doted over him and enjoyed every moment with him. When she perceived that Ishmael was taking advantage of Isaac, she compelled Abraham to expel Hagar and Ishmael from the household. Only Isaac was to be Abraham's true heir and successor.

Sarah loved Isaac with a total love. Indeed, Isaac could not fail to realize that the only person in the world he could fully trust was his mother Sarah. Hagar and Ishmael were certainly not to be relied upon. After the Akeidah, Isaac must surely have had misgivings about trusting his father Abraham, who had raised a knife to his throat.

When Sarah died, Isaac felt very alone in the universe. There was no one who loved him with an unqualified love. There was no one who understood him fully. There was no one to whom he could turn for genuine consolation. So he mourned for three years. He felt lost and abandoned.

But even more painful than being unloved by anyone, Isaac had no one whom he himself loved with a full love. A loveless life is a tragic life, a life of perpetual mourning.

And then Rebeccah enters the scene. "And Rebeccah lifted up her eyes, and when she saw Isaac she alighted from the camel ... and she took her veil and covered herself (24:65)." Abraham's servant explained to Isaac that Rebeccah had been chosen to become Isaac's wife.

Instead of hesitating nervously, Isaac suddenly came to life. He was immediately impressed with Rebeccah's modest and respectful behavior. This was a dramatic instance of love at first sight. Lonely Isaac now had love in his life again. Lonely Rebeccah – and she must have been lonely coming to a new land to start a new life among people she did not know – saw in Isaac a meditative, sensitive man – a man worthy of her love.

Isaac was consoled on the loss of his mother. He saw in Rebeccah those special qualities that had characterized Sarah. More than that, he found in Rebeccah the love which had been absent from his life since Sarah's death. He was now able to deal with Sarah's death because he now had a future with Rebeccah. He could redirect his thoughts to moving his life forward instead of grieving for an irretrievable past.

I have often told mourners: You never get over the death of a loved one; but you learn to get through it. The deceased loved ones remain with us "qualitatively" as long as we live. We treasure our memories of their lives, and we carry those memories with us as we forge our ways into the future. We find consolation not by forgetting them, but by bringing them along with us every day of our lives.

We find consolation through the power of love, the blessing of loving and being loved.

-Rabbi Marc D. Angel

Chapter Three

FINDING GOD IN THE DARK

Possibly the four most devastating words to many mourners are "It was God's will." Spoken to comfort, instead, for many they open yet another wound. If God hovers over us and cares for us, why would God ever will that so much pain come upon us? Wouldn't God want to protect and shield us? The loss of a loved one is so unfair, even unjust. A God of justice simply wouldn't behave this way!

In our time of grief, we may feel that God has never been farther from us than at that moment. In reality, though, God has never been closer. We are not in a position to debate the theological fairness of suffering and death; we simply don't know enough. God, and even the natural world, remain to a large extent beyond our human comprehension. How, then, is God close to us, and how can we find God in these most difficult moments in our lives? In any way that comfort comes, God comes with that comfort. Across time, cultures, family traditions and individual understanding, consolation is God's mission, undertaken in the many ways that humans find comfort.

The Talmud (b. Sotah 14a) notes that God personally illustrated the ways in which God wants us to comfort each other, by caring for the poor (clothing Adam and Eve), visiting the sick (appearing to Abraham after his circumcision), burying the dead (God buried Moses) and comforting mourners (God blessed Isaac after his father's death). In doing these things, we ourselves show the comforting Presence of God, which seems so invisible without our aid.

God is Everywhere

Throughout our Torah literature and liturgy, we use numerous different names to refer to Hashem, depending upon which of His attributes is being highlighted. The name used here, "*HaMakom*," the Omnipresent, suggests that God is indeed everywhere, even in those places and at those times when we may not readily sense His presence. In fact, it is specifically on those occasions when we may think that God is far away from us and perhaps has even abandoned us entirely that we are reminded, by referring to Him with this particular name, that in truth He is still very much with us in our midst.

We thus find, for example, that a mourner, who certainly feels as though God has turned away from him, is to be consoled with a phrase that uses this name ("May the Omnipresent console you").

-Yom Kippur Mahzor with Commentary
Adapted from the Teachings of Rabbi Joseph B. Soloveitchik, pp. 64, 65

♦♦♦

Oh God, give me strength to forget
evils over and done,
history's falls and failings,
yesterday's frozen hope.

And give me strength to keep watch
for fair weather after a stormy day,
incense of flowers
and quiet waves.

God give me strength to wait
and time to hope;
until the last day
strength to keep watch and rejoice
as doves are hatched and babes are born,
as flowers bud and blossom
and visions break out and grow.

Give me strength, O God.

-Eliezer Bugatin

Stand Up Straight

God's first words to the prophet Ezekiel are: "Son of man, stand on your feet that I may speak to you" (Ezek. 2:1). Reaching

♦ 73 ♦

our full human height we are most ready to encounter God.

When a Jew has suffered a loss and tears a garment in mourning, the tearing takes place while the mourner stands upright. Confronting the pain and puzzlement of loss, standing upright signifies dignity and hope.

The central Jewish prayer is called the *Amidah*, literally "the standing." Although we bow during the prayer, our posture for most of its duration is upright. Above the ark in many synagogues is carved the injunction "Know before whom you stand."

Judaism does not scorn acceptance and submission. That is the reality of any fragile human being – there is much we cannot change, or have not the wisdom to change. But we face the world standing. Judaism enshrines the satiric wisdom of Monty Python: God appears out of the sky in the Holy Grail movie and pleads with the obsequious knights to "Stop groveling!" God, our tradition teaches, wants our full, vibrant, vivid capable selves, standing ready to heal an anguished world. We cannot know our own limitations until we test our own strength. When the child, stretched to full height, proudly proclaims, "Look how tall I've grown!" she is following an ancient tradition. In a broken world, we stand ready to serve.

-Rabbi David Wolpe

♦♦♦

I thank You, God, for the glory of late days and the excellent face of Your sun. I thank You for good news received. I thank You for the pleasures I have enjoyed and for those I have been able to confer. And now, when the clouds gather and the rain impends, permit me not to be cast down; let me not lose the savor of the past mercies and past pleasures; but, like the voice of a bird singing in the rain, let grateful memory survive in the hour of darkness.

-Robert Louis Stevenson

The Shape of Human Hearts

The human heart is not a sculpture. It is a mosaic.

Our hearts resemble stained-glass windows. You can see where the pieces are joined, the cracks and fissures. But soldered together they let in light and cast radiant images. There is a composite beauty.

Life offers great joy alongside overwhelming sadness. At times we are moved to neglect one or the other, to speak only of enjoying God's blessings, or to shake our fists at the sky in fury for all the pain.

To hold joy or sorrow alone oversimplifies the stained glass, multi-hued heart. Hearts that are too defended in this world, that avoid being hurt or broken, end up worn and wasted, in the way that an old, rusted clock, unpolished, unwound, uncherished, will no longer run. When the Talmudic Rabbi Alexandri defined the difference between God and human beings he did not speak in terms of power, or creativity or eternity. People, he said, are ashamed to use broken vessels. God cares only for broken vessels.

We are those broken vessels. Our promise is in that brokenness, that beauty. The light shines through the fragments of each shattered, treasured heart.

-Rabbi David Wolpe

When We Can't Understand

As human beings, we want so much to understand everything that is going on in our lives. We'd like to see everything that has happened and everything that will happen in a neat box all tied up with a pretty ribbon. However, God doesn't work that way. You can't place God in a box. Our God is way too big and far too great to be contained. He works in ways that we can't possibly comprehend. As it says in Proverbs 20:24, "A person's steps are directed by the Lord. How then can anyone understand their own way?" No, we can't understand how God works – and that's a good thing.

If we could understand God's ways, then His actions would be limited to our intellectual capabilities. I don't know about you, but I want a God who is limited by nothing! A colleague of mine once put it this way: "I don't want to pray to a God who I can understand!" I want God to have ways to make things happen in my life when I don't see a way. I want a God who can make sense out of my messy life when I can't see a way to clean it up myself. I want a God who is bigger and smarter than me!

Friends, let's remember that when we go through things in life that we can't understand, it's OK. We don't have to understand. God understands and that's all that matters. As it says in Proverb 3:5-6, "Trust in the Lord ... lean not on your own understanding ... and he will make your paths straight."

-Rabbi Yechiel Eckstein

The Masterpiece of Sorrow

The book of Job is sunk in sorrow. It tells the troubling story of a man tested by every misfortune, including the egregious speeches of his friends, who manages nonetheless to keep faith. Job refuses to turn away from the God who has turned away from him.

Throughout the generations many explanations have been given to account for the message of this soaring, vexing work. For a moment, however, let us consider the author, whoever he (or she) may have been. Here was a person well acquainted with affliction, who knew the varied trails and travails of the human heart. Doubtless the author had himself suffered loss – everyone does, and in the ancient world, loss was more immediate and uncushioned.

What did our author do? Turned suffering to song. Rather than brood in silence, the author of Job created a masterwork to console others. Robert Frost said that poetry was made of griefs, not grievances. In the book of Job, a poet, summoning his griefs, draws us into the ambit of pain to help us understand our own loss and struggle for faith. For centuries the sad, sick, and bereft have turned the pages of this magnificent work, and found a spirit who expresses the anguish in all our hearts.

-Rabbi David Wolpe

How Long the Night?

My soul is in deep anguish. How long, Lord, how long?

-Psalm 6:3

Many times in life we are faced with challenges and

hardships. While these times may be difficult, even painful to endure, they are certainly not without meaning and purpose. King Solomon, the wisest of all men, taught: "The crucible for silver and the furnace for gold, but the LORD tests the heart" (Proverbs 17:3). Just as precious metals like gold and silver are produced through the furnace and the crucible, so, too, our hearts are purified through our trials and tribulations.

Often, the most difficult aspect of going through hard times is not knowing when it will end. Going through a dark tunnel is not so bad when we can see the light shining through the other side. But when there is no end in sight, we have to rely on our faith that our difficulties won't last forever. Still, the heart aches as we wonder when the darkness will finally end.

King David spoke to this in Psalm 6. He wrote: "My soul is in deep anguish. How long, LORD, how long?" David was in pain and he wanted to know when it would end. Later in the psalm, he said: "I am worn out from my groaning. All night long I flood my bed with weeping ..." (v.6). David was tired and weary as we often are during our own difficult times. Maybe it is a prolonged illness or a lengthy period of financial insecurity. It could be a chronic relationship problem or repeated professional failure. It's difficult going through trials day after day for a long period of time. It's a true test of spiritual and mental endurance.

So what kept David going through his long night of distress?

It was knowing that everything can change in an instant; salvation can come in one moment. At the end of the psalm, David wrote that all his enemies would "suddenly be put to shame" (v.10).Unexpectedly, everything can turn around – when the time is just right.

Friends, when our dark night seems long and unending, we need to remember that it can end suddenly, too. Salvation can be just around the corner. But more importantly, we need to know that there is a purpose to our suffering and a reason why it may be drawn out. Pastor Rick Warren said it beautifully: "God changes caterpillars into butterflies, sand into pearls, and coal into diamonds using TIME and PRESSURE. He's working on you, too."

Only God knows how long the night will be. But we get to

determine who we will be when the dawn finally arrives.
    With prayers for shalom, peace,

                                              -Rabbi Yechiel Eckstein

The Plan of the Master Weaver

Our lives are but fine weavings,
That God and we prepare,
Each life becomes a fabric planned,
And fashioned in God's care.

We may not always see just how,
The weavings intertwine,
But we must trust the Master's hand,
And follow God's design.

For God can view the pattern,
Upon the upper side,
While we must look from underneath,
And trust in God to guide.

Sometimes a strand of sorrow
Is added to the plan,
And though it is difficult for us,
We still must understand,
That it's God who moves the shuttle,
Who knows what's best,
So we must weave in patience,
And leave to God the rest ...

Not till the loom is silent,
And the shuttles cease to fly,
Shall God unroll the canvas
And explain the reason why-
The dark threads are as needed
In the Weaver's skillful hand,
As the threads of gold and silver,
In the pattern God has planned.

                                              -Anonymous

A Short Visit-For a Divine Purpose

Strange is our situation here on earth. Each of us comes for a short visit, not knowing why, yet sometimes seeming to a divine purpose. There is one thing we do know definitively: that we are here for the sake of each other.

Many times a day I realize how much my own outer and inner life is built upon the labor of others, and how earnestly I must exert myself in order to give in return as much as I have received and am still receiving.

-Albert Einstein

The Storm

A little girl walked to and from school daily. Though the weather that morning was questionable and clouds were forming, she made her daily trek to the elementary school.

As the afternoon progressed, the winds whipped up, along with thunder and lightning. The mother of the little girl felt concerned that her daughter would be frightened as she walked home from school and she herself feared that the electrical storm might harm her child.

Following the roar of thunder, lightning, like a flaming sword, would cut through the sky. Full of concern, the mother quickly got into her car and drove along the route to her child's school.

As she did so, she saw her little girl walking along, but at each flash of lightning, the child would stop, look up and smile. Another and another were to follow quickly and with each the little girl would look at the streak of light and smile.

When the mother's car drove up beside the child she lowered the window and called to her, "What are you doing? Why do you keep stopping?"

The child answered, "I am trying to look pretty, God keeps taking my picture."

-Unknown

The Bridge Is Love

In Thornton Wilder's 1927 novel, "The Bridge of San Luis

Rey", he tells of a rope bridge over a deep gorge in a small Peruvian village that suddenly collapses, sending five people to their deaths. A young Catholic priest, Brother Juniper, witnesses the tragedy and becomes obsessed with the question of why God would let it happen. He researches the lives of the five unrelated, seemingly random victims and learns that each of them had recently resolved a relationship issue in his or her life, and each of them had learned what it means to love someone. Brother Juniper's conclusion: We are put on earth to love, and when we have done that, we have fulfilled our mission. The book concludes: "Soon we shall die and all memory of those five will have left the earth. We ourselves shall be loved for a while and forgotten. But the love will have been enough... There is a land of the living and land of the dead, and the bridge is love, the only survival, the only meaning."

-Rabbi Steven Saltzman

The Greatest Compensation

How many of us perform our small acts of charity and goodness for the wrong reasons. We expect a kind deed to be rewarded by a kind fate, to preserve us from trouble and misfortune. More than once have I heard this melancholy verdict: "When my mother died, I stopped believing in God. She was such a good person, how could God let this happen to her?"

Goodness does not confer immunity to disease, disaster, or death. It does not guarantee a life without trouble or tragedy. These are the common lot of all of us.

Is there then no reward for living a life of rectitude and uprightness? There is, indeed. We are rewarded not for our good deeds but by our good deeds. The reward for doing good is becoming a better human being. The greatest compensation for any good deed is simply to have done it. It is inherent in the act itself. Moses Maimonides, the twelfth-century Jewish philosopher, gave us the right reason for doing the right deed: "It is not enough to serve God in the hope of future reward. One must do right and avoid wrong because one is a human and owes it to one's humanity to seek perfection."

-Rabbi Sidney Greenberg

God Is Now Here

There are people who emerge from an encounter with grief richer human beings, taller in stature, more compassionate, more sensitive, more appreciative of the gift of life. They can say with the poet William Wordsworth: "A deep distress hath humanized my soul."

The same fire that melts the butter hardens the egg. The same wind that extinguishes a match will fan a flame into a stronger blaze. Humans do not live by facts alone.

An aggressive atheist in a mood to advertise his point of view painted these words on a roadside billboard: "God is nowhere." A seven-year-old girl riding in the family car passed the billboard. She was thrilled and excited, for she read these words: "God is now here."

-Rabbi Sidney Greenberg

Visualization: Let There Be Light

There was total darkness in the world until the Creator said, "Let there be light." The Torah states this at the very beginning, said the Chofetz Chaim, to tell us that even in the darkest periods of life, in a flash the Almighty can create light. Repeating these words will bring much light into your life.

Let the image of serene light be a source of creating positive energy for you. Visualize white light going from your head to your toes. Feel all your muscles relaxing. Feel every cell in your body vibrating with healthy energy. Feel that healthy energy cycling again and again. Let this empower you.

-Rabbi Zelig Pliskin

To Hold with Open Arms

After Rabbi Milton Steinberg recovered following his heart attack he walked out into the bright midday sun. He thought, "How precious – how careless." Life is so precious and we are so careless with it. How can we pay so little heed when we know that everything cherished must end? Perhaps we fear that if we care too much, the losses of life will be unbearable.

Building from that moment Steinberg wrote that we

should hold life dear, but because we realize that everything is temporary, we cannot hold it too close. How do we live knowing that all we find so wondrous, so beautiful, can be gone in an instant? This is how Steinberg concludes in words written more than half a century ago: "And only with God can we ease the intolerable tension of our existence. For only when He is given, can we hold life at once infinitely precious and yet as a thing lightly to be surrendered. Only because of Him is it possible for us to clasp the world, but with relaxed hands; to embrace it, but with open arms."

Remember Steinberg's legacy: the wisdom to cherish and to let go. The wisdom of holding with open arms.

-Rabbi David Wolpe

An Answer to Evil

The great question of why God permits evil is usually treated in Judaism less as a "why" question than as a "what" question: Given the evil in the world, what do we do about it?

We can wonder about God's role, but it is ultimately inscrutable. We cannot know. Imagine how little a two-year-old understands an adult. He cannot even understand what he does not know. The Jewish tradition conceives of the gap between humans and God as far greater than that between an adult and an infant. So how, ultimately, can we understand?

What we can do, is act. Faced with evil, we can choose goodness. In a weary world, *mitzvot* enable us to begin closing the breach between what is and what should be. Even in the most difficult circumstance, we can choose. As the great Viktor Frankl writes in Man's Search for Meaning: "We who lived in concentration camps can remember the men who walked through the huts comforting others, giving away their last piece of bread. They may have been few in number, but they offer sufficient proof that everything can be taken from a man but one thing: the last of the human freedoms – to choose one's attitude in any given set of circumstances, to choose one's own way.

-Rabbi David Wolpe

Chapter Four

KADDISH: ALONE TOGETHER

All this came upon us,
   yet we have not forgotten you;
   we have not been false to Your covenant.
Our hearts have not turned back;
   our feet have not strayed from Your path.
Though You crushed us and made us a haunt
for jackals;
   You covered us over with deep darkness ...

We are brought down to the dust;
   our bodies cling to the ground.
Rise up and help us;
   rescue us because of Your unfailing love.

-Psalm 44:18-20; 25-26

Jewish law and tradition dictate that people should come together at times of mourning. Communal gatherings for funerals and shiva, the traditional seven days of mourning after burial during which close relatives remain indoors, visited and cared for by the community, begin this togetherness. As we proceed along the path of our grief, other rituals gradually re-integrate us into the routines of our daily lives. But room is left to remember our dead, and the Jewish tradition of the Mourner's Kaddish allows us ritual space to work through our grief.

The Kaddish does not mention death at all. It speaks of the greatness of God. It lifts us from our painful presence and encourages us to see the beauty and majesty of God's world again, softens our hearts toward God, and calls us insistently to be with others. Traditionally, ten Jewish adults, a minyan, must come together for the Kaddish to be said, generally in the context of a prayer service. We even name our services after this requirement – "It's almost time for minyan!" One of the sources below describes a famous sculpture in the Diaspora Museum in Tel Aviv, Israel, entitled "The Minyan", depicting a group of nine, waiting for the tenth so that prayer may commence, inviting the viewer to be included. However alone we feel, in the context of Kaddish, we are needed by others as much as we need them.

For many reasons, not every mourner is in a position to follow this traditional practice. Therefore, we include passages here with suggestions for other practices that might assist mourners who cannot or do not wish to say Kaddish.

Embracing Farewell

I said Kaddish three times a day for the eleven months of mourning [for my father's death]. According to Jewish tradition, in the year after you die you are undergoing judgment by the heavenly tribunal. … During this year of judgment, whatever your mourners do that is good – giving *tzedakah*, charity, or performing any other religious act, such as leading services – accrues to the merit of your case.

Most people, however, do not know enough Hebrew to lead services. This has been true throughout Jewish history, and this is how the Kaddish, which has nothing to do with death, became the prayer for the dead. The Kaddish occurs at every point of transition between the various parts of the prayer service and is not in Hebrew, but in Aramaic, the language Jews spoke when the Kaddish originated. Since it was in the spoken language of its day, it was the one prayer in the service everyone could read, so reading it became a way mourners who did not know Hebrew could fulfill the obligation of performing a religious act in order to accumulate merit for a dead relative. Of course, it is far better for a mourner to lead the whole service.

I was so involved in getting the service right that I hardly thought of my father as I led the prayers and repeated the Kaddish. The words of the Kaddish glorified God; they did nothing, as far as I could see, to remind me that my father was, in fact, dead. But even though the Kaddish did not originate as a prayer for the dead, there are some after-the-fact explanations for how, in a subtle way, it nonetheless actually is. One midrash, one Jewish legend, explains that whenever anyone dies, God is diminished, so when you say *Yitgadal...*, magnified..., the words are working to address this loss, to increase God, as it were. Another midrash points out that the death of a loved one is precisely the moment you want to curse God. The words of the Kaddish, which affirm God and God's role in the world, help to put a brake on this anger. Indeed, that is exactly the way my sister had reacted when our father had taken his last desperate labored breath. She had cursed God, crying and screaming. But I hadn't cried. I hadn't cried at all.

What I had done was set out punctiliously to observe the laws of mourning. In the eleven months of mourning, I did not miss a single day of saying Kaddish for my father, though I rarely thought of him while saying the words. And then the last day of mourning arrived. It was then, as I began to say the Kaddish for the last time, that I saw my father at the beginning of the prayer, asking me to say these words for him: *Yitgadal v'yitkadash* ... All these months, without my knowing it, we had, in fact, been holding on to each other inside these words. Now the end of the words was coming into view – *aleinu ve-al chol Yisrael* – the moment when I must bow farewell, to the left and to the right, and step back out of this prayer where my arms were around my father and his arms were around me. I had to let go.

They led me sobbing from the bimah.

-Rabbi Alan Lew

Kaddish College

A helpful way of thinking about this part of the grief journey is through Rabbi Zalman Schachter-Shalomi's concept of *"Kaddish* College." Reb Zalman describes *Kaddish* as a psycho-spiritual process during which one works toward deep resolution with a parent or another who has died. He tells about a conversation he had with his deceased father:

After my father died, I was driving from Boulder back to Winnipeg, where I was living at the time. In those years I drove a truck, and as I was getting on the highway someone cut me off. I rolled down the window and let out a string of curses –

Polish, Yiddish – every obscenity in my vocabulary. As I did that I could hear the echoing of my father's voice. It was exactly as he would curse and swear while driving at the wheel. Shaken up, I stopped the truck, and said aloud, "Papa, this is one of yours! This one you can have back." I realized that I was just beginning to sort out my *yerishah,* my inheritance from Papa. In saying that to him, it dawned on me that I could now claim as my own what his legacy was to me, keep all the good stuff I had been given, and reject what was his, not mine, and no longer useful in my life.

-Jewish Pastoral Care

The Secret of the Kaddish

The Kaddish may be the best known Jewish prayer and yet its purpose is mysterious. Though the mourning prayer, it makes no mention of death. Rather, what it proclaims is the greatness and sanctity of God and God's name.

There are many sources and explanations for this enigma. The most common is that at a moment of loss, the affirmation of God's greatness reminds us of ultimate justice. Another explanation resorts to history: since the earliest recitation of the Kaddish was not tied to mourning, but rather to study, the prayer became accidentally associated with death.

This just touches the surface of many ingenious and beautiful explanations. But I want to repeat something I heard in the name of Rabbi Shlomo Carlebach that struck me as almost inexpressibly beautiful and moving. Noting that the Kaddish is about the greatness of God, Rabbi Carlebach said that the prayer is what those who have died would say to us could they speak from where they were. So at the moment of loss we realize that our loved ones – who now know the secrets of what follows this life – are reassuring us about the greatness of God and the kindness of the fate that awaits us all.

-Rabbi David Wolpe

The Minyan

The late Abba Kovner, hero of the Vilna Ghetto, resistance fighter, organizer of Brichah, the illegal rescue of hundreds of thousands of Jewish refugees of the Holocaust to Israel, also poet and writer, was one of the founders of Bet Ha-Tfutzot, the Diaspora Museum at Tel Aviv University. Kovner, himself, designed one special corner of the museum, known as "The Minyan". The exhibit consists of nine wax figures, representing Jews from all over the world, praying together.

Of course, there is an apparent problem with this exhibit. A minyan is ten, not nine. Abba Kovner explained, how, after the war, in Israel, living on a Kibbutz, he felt very alone. He missed all of his family, friends, and fellow fighters who fell in the war, and grieved for the thousands already lost in the battle to establish Israel. In that time of aloneness, a Jew approached Kovner, asking him to be the tenth in a minyan. Kovner, not a religious Jew by any stretch of the imagination, agreed, and became the tenth. And that seemingly trivial moment in his life changed him forever, for it taught him that he was not alone, that he was part of the larger minyan of *K'lal Yisrael*, that he belonged to something far greater than himself.

And so, why only nine figures in the exhibit at the Diaspora Museum? Kovner wanted the viewer, the visitor, to become that tenth, to know that the exhibit, indeed, the nation, would not be complete, would not be a functional whole, without his, without her involvement.

We too, have to be part of that sacred minyan. We have to do what history demands of us, we have to secure our presence in the eternal minyan of the people of Israel.

-Rabbi Philip Scheim

Moving On: When Kaddish Ends

A Kaddish vision ...

I am an astronaut on a space walk, floating in space while tethered to the mothership. It is an image familiar to all of us who grew up with America's space program. I am floating freely in the weightlessness of space, but also holding on to the hand of my mother who has died. She is not tethered to anything, and is connected to me only by the grasp of my hand. I know that the second I let go of her hand she'll drift off, moving ever farther away into the void of deep space. But the ship's commander is telling me that it's time to come back in, and to do so, I must let go of my mother.

And then I stop daydreaming.

The end of my year of Kaddish for my late mother Lillian Skolnik, *aleha hashalom,* is at hand. I can't say that the time has passed quickly, but the prospect of ending Kaddish has obviously played games with my subconscious.

To take the Kaddish responsibility seriously is to know its capacity to slow life down. The incessant need to be near an available minyan is unrelenting, and invades every moment of one's consciousness. That is, I would suppose, exactly what it is supposed to do. Vacations and days off are planned around it, and business appointments, too. When you live in a densely populated Jewish area like central Queens, as I do, you learn exactly when and where all the available morning, afternoon and evening services are. Learning to factor them into your schedule becomes almost like a game. "I can catch the 3:30 p.m. Mincha there, and then the 11:30 p.m. Ma'ariv there," and you feel quite accomplished when you make it through a complicated day without missing a service.

And so it is that, as I prepared to end this stage of grieving for my mother, I found myself wondering, what now?

On the one hand, I was more than ready to be relieved of the Kaddish responsibility, and the mourning rituals that go with it. I miss live music terribly, and have a list of movies that I'd still love to try and catch on a screen bigger than my television. And even though I was a regular at morning and evening minyan before my mother died and will be long after my formal mourning, I must admit that one of the first things I promised myself after the Kaddish is over was a morning to sleep late. Sounds trivial, I know, but not when you haven't done it in a year.

On the other hand, I am loath to cede the right to be focused on my loss, and my memories, three times a day. Most people have a very short attention span when it comes to listening to other people's pain. That's not a good thing or a bad thing – just a truth. But God's attention span is, as it were, timeless. God never tires of our tears, or our sadness. When I sat in synagogue morning, afternoon and evening and was alone with my sense of loss, I was not really alone. I was with God who is the healer of broken hearts, and all year it felt as if God waits for me to welcome me. God never says to me "it's time to move on."

And yet it is.

I have counseled countless people through their grieving process during the years of my rabbinate. I couldn't possibly begin to count the number of times I have told them that time will ultimately bring them healing in ways that they cannot possibly imagine in the here and now. And it's true, of course. Time is the great healer, and learning to feel the presence of God while at prayer is a great salve for deep heartache. I have also counseled people to use the synagogue as a safe space for their grief. No one will ever ask you to leave the synagogue for crying during a service.

I understand all this now more than ever. "Moving on" is not the same as letting go. It's about coming back into the rhythm of life with gusto, and reclaiming the capacity to know and experience the joy of living with a full heart.

In order to do this, I also understand that I must re-enter the mothership and let go of my mother's hand. The Commander is telling me that it's time. Yes, it hurts to let go. The end of my Kaddish is a final, irreducible goodbye. But Ecclesiastes taught us long ago that love is as strong as death, and it endures beyond the realm of the physical. It is, indeed, time to move on ... and to remember.

-Rabbi Gerald Skolnik

Voice From Heaven

It's raining outside, and I am pedaling my exercise bike when I suddenly hear a loud voice addressing me.

"Is that you, rabbi?" I look up. Has the pedaling pushed me beyond the border of sanity?

"What do you want?" I ask.

"Rabbi, do you remember the Yahrzeit list last week?"

"The Yahrzeit list," I stutter, "You mean every name on it?"

"No, I mean my name."

At that point, I stop pedaling and begin listening.

"I died two years ago, and I am bewildered. Sure, my kids

are busy and successful, but wouldn't you think they could spare a couple of hours to come to synagogue and give thanks for my life? Is it too much to ask for them to be there when you pronounce my name?

"Perhaps ..." I interrupt, but to no avail. This soul is on fire.

"I admit that I wasn't a perfect parent. We had our ups and downs, but I loved them. I nurtured them, worried about them, and my heart broke at their defeats and rejoiced at their happiness. So why do they allow my name to be read with no one there to remember me, to smile at the thought of me, to fill with the love of me?"

"Maybe they were out of town," I respond seeking an excuse for my congregants.

"You're wrong!" says the voice. "From my heavenly perch, I see and hear it all. Last year they were out playing golf. This year, despite the letter sent them from synagogue, they forgot my Yahrzeit completely, didn't even light a candle at home."

"But they probably think of you all the time," I say.

"Of course they do! But that's different. You love your wife and you're with her all the time. Do you use that as an excuse for not celebrating her birthday or your anniversary?"

I nod, and the voice continues.

"I am talking about devoting some special time, some time that flows out of love, to my memory. That's what saying Kaddish is about. It's not much to ask. And from out there in the pure air of heaven, it's what keeps us souls living!"

With that the voice disappeared, and I rushed to my desk to write down this report.

-Rabbi Harvey Fields

A Special Prayer For Those
Not Saying Yizkor For Parents

The following prayer may be recited by worshipers who are blessed by having their parents still living while others are reciting Yizkor:

ALMIGHTY GOD, while those who have lost their parents and their dear ones call to mind those who have gone to their eternal rest, I at this solemn moment raise my eyes unto You, the Giver of Life, and from a grateful heart thank You for Your mercies in having preserved the life of my beloved father and mother.

MAY it be Your will, Adonai my God and the God of my ancestors, to bless them with health and strength, so that they may be with me for many years to come. Bless them even as they have blessed me, and guard them even as they have guarded me.

IN return for all their affection and the sacrifices which they have made for me, may I bring them joy and lighten their cares. May it be my privilege to help them in every way that lies within my power; may I learn to understand and recognize the duty I owe unto them, that I may never have cause to reproach myself when it is too late.

SHIELD my home from all sorrow. May peace and harmony and Your spirit ever reign within its walls. Keep me true to You and to all with whom I come in contact so that I may do Your will with a perfect heart, my Creator in Heaven. *Amen.*

-Adapted from South African Mahzor

How To Remember Loved Ones
When You Can't Say Kaddish

For many people it is not always possible to fulfill the complete regiment of Mourner's Kaddish three times each day for a whole year. Others seek out a way to memorialize a loved one for whom they have no formal obligation to say Kaddish, but for whom they wish to honor in this way nevertheless. Rabbi Sue Fendrick came up with a creative substitute, which is in conformity with the *Halakhah* according to most authorities, even for an immediate relative when saying Kaddish is impossible. Here is her story:

As a rabbi on a college campus, I am often approached by students in relationship to a death which would ordinarily not require Kaddish-saying – grandparents, uncles. Occasionally, non-Jewish students ask a similar question. All of them are looking for something regular. (A grandchild can say Kaddish if the child is not, but usually my students are not looking to do that either.)

When my mother was four, in pre-war Poland, she contracted typhoid fever. She was supposed to be quarantined, but my grandparents smuggled her to a better hospital farther away. She lapsed into a coma and eventually regained consciousness, but for a month my grandparents were hardly able to see her. My grandfather was beside himself. An "alte yid," an old Jew, a beggar, to whom my grandfather had given money, told him to recite Psalm 20 (which appears after *Ashrei* and before *Uva liTzion* – which I will forever pronounce OO-va l- TZEE – on in his memory – in weekday Shacharit). My mother recovered. It became our family Psalm.

When I was saying Kaddish for my grandfather, I said this *perek tehillim* when I couldn't get to a minyan. It made a big difference to have something regular "*bimkom Kaddish*." I often recommend this to anyone from a biblical faith tradition who is looking for a regular practice in the wake of mourning.

On a related subject, each year on my grandfather's Yahrzeit I have had a learning evening, called "Life is a School. Whenever I asked him – he who had an eighth grade education – where he learned this Latin phrase or that interesting fact about French history – he answered, "What? Life – life is a school!"

The first year, I taught Midrash Mishle on *Eshet Chayil* (Zayde z"l used to say about Mishle, "Read it, *mamenyu*, read it – there are deep taughts [sic] in there!") Year 2, I asked everyone to bring something, anything, to teach for 5 minutes. There was Mishnah, theater exercises, psychiatric epidemiology, bats, a midrash on Bezalel and his grandchildren, etc. Year 3, I taught niggunim. Year 4, like Year 2. Year 5, I taught zemirot. Year 6, we did something slightly different and went to the Hebrew Home for the Aged to sing to the residents.

My friends look forward to it every year. It is a wonderful, wonderful way to remember someone on an annual basis.

-Rabbi Susan Fendrick

The Rest Is Up To Me

In his popular book, "*Kaddish*", Leon Wieseltier, writer for

The New Republic, reflects on the role that the synagogue plays in his spiritual life, especially during recitation of the Mourner's Kaddish ("*Kaddish Yatom*"). He writes:

"It occurred to me today that I might spend a whole year in shul, morning prayers, afternoon prayers, evening prayers and never have a religious experience. A discouraging notion. Yet I must not ask for what cannot be given. Shul was not invented for a religious experience. In shul, a religious experience is an experience of religion. The rest is up to me."

Too often we expect the synagogue to do for us what we should be doing for ourselves. The aura of the recitation of the *Kaddish Yatom* in the synagogue setting is a powerful one, but we must open our hearts to let it in.

-D.P.E.

In the Year of Mourning

Most mornings now, I wake up with the sounds of Kaddish in my head.

It's not surprising. For the last seven weeks, my psyche has been focused on the traditional mourners' prayer, which I've been reciting at least six times a day in my mother's memory.

My life seems to revolve around, and focus on, getting to synagogue on time – morning, afternoon and evening – being prepared to lead the services, and concentrating my thoughts on the concept of elevating my mother's soul through the recitation of Kaddish.

It's a new and compelling routine, but I'm not complaining. In fact, I think the approach our rabbis devised for mourning a close relative is brilliant psychologically, first separating us from the normal responsibilities of our daily life for the week of shiva, and then gradually restoring us to "normal" life through an extended period of less intense but restrictive mourning – 30 days for a spouse, sibling or a child, and 11 months for a parent, one who gave us life.

At a time when one is vulnerable to depression and a profound sense of loss, the mitzvah of Kaddish – the ancient Aramaic prayer that praises God and makes no mention of death – gives the mourner a sense of purpose, the feeling he or she is able to do something tangible for the loved one. When the inclination may be to withdraw and turn inward, we are given a task to fulfill that involves being with others, taking part in a minyan three times a day and reciting a prayer that, according to tradition, benefits the soul.

The ritual expression a fellow congregant might greet you with after hearing you chant the Kaddish – "may the *neshama* [soul] have an aliyah [literally, an elevation]" – is profound.

It underscores the belief that we in this world still have a connection with and active role to play in the fate of our departed relative, whose spirit can be raised and enhanced by our prayers. And the expression suggests to me that our own *neshama,* too, can be lifted through the experience, making us more compassionate, reflective and humble in the face of life's realities.

There are countless laws and customs associated with the year of mourning, from not shaving for the first 30 days (as if I needed an outward sign of my grief) to moving one's seat further back in synagogue to refraining from social situations.

Rabbis have various interpretations about how strictly to adhere to, say, not listening to music, or going to the theater or movies, weddings or parties for the year. They sometimes distinguish between public events and private enjoyment, like watching a film at home rather than going out to a movie theater, or determine how many couples, if any, one can share a meal with on Shabbat. So far I've been listening for my mother's voice in my head to guide me, and it's been working. "Be respectful, but don't overdo it," she would say. And "think about other people's feelings."

That includes seeking out fellow mourners in the synagogue, as we are a lonely group, by definition, a part of the congregation yet also apart. Ours is an exclusive club of sorts, bound by loss, yet at some point in life everyone becomes a member. In the 24 years since I observed the year of mourning for my father, I've increased my admiration for regular shul-goers, who attend services daily, year in and year out. And I recall that a kind word, a smile, a recognition of another mourner's status can go a long way toward easing the sense of isolation – for both of you.

One friend who knew my mother told me he is grateful when he hears me say Kaddish because it brings back warm memories of her for him. That comment was such a comfort, and deeply appreciated.

My brother and I have been sharing our thoughts – a comfort in itself – and comparing our shul-going experiences. I'm grateful to be acknowledged by others after leading the service or reciting the Kaddish, but it doesn't always happen.

I still haven't come up with a proper response when people ask, "how are you doing?" They mean well, but what am I supposed to say? That I am still in a bit of a fog, but doing the best I can? Not only is every day different, but one's mood can change in a heartbeat. There are moments when I can tell a story about my mother and smile at the memory. Other times I can be at work at my desk or riding home on the bus and a vivid recollection of my mom – of a simple image or the sound of her voice – will come to me out of the blue and bring tears to my eyes.

And there are questions from my young grandchildren that I can't answer. Where is Bubbe now? Can she still see me? Can she hear me if I talk to her? Will I ever see her again?

In their innocence, they articulate the imponderables that we adults grapple with but have learned to avoid asking, even of ourselves.

My year of mourning has a long way to go, I've only just started on this journey that connects the past to the present. I take each day as it comes, emotionally exhausted at times from the awareness of my fragile state or just worrying about the next minyan, but grateful for the opportunities for prayer and reflection and especially for the mitzvah of saying Kaddish for my mother.

May I be worthy of honoring her good name, always. And may the *neshama* have an aliyah.

-Gary Rosenblatt

From Death to Life, From Darkness to Light

Each morning and each evening, the people of the shul's daily minyan gather for prayer. It isn't exciting. The melodies aren't particularly uplifting. Sometimes there is a word of learning, but no sermon – none of the flourishes, trappings and trimmings of professional homiletics. The poetry of prayer is often murmured in the rapid-fire rhythm of traditional *davening*. And at the end of the service, most of the minyan rises to recite Kaddish – in memory of a loved one recently departed or recalled at this Yahrzeit. It isn't exciting. But in its own way, it is profoundly moving and deeply spiritual.

Spirituality today has come to mean emotional experiences of ecstasy and wonder – peak moments revealing the Presence of God in stirring song, powerful words, and the uplift of a responsive community. These are true and significant experiences. But there are other kinds of spirituality. The spirituality of the minyan isn't ecstatic or exuberant. The spiritual genius of the minyan is located in a deep experience of the steady, regular unchanging rhythms of life. This is a spirituality of constancy and continuity. It is unexciting and unremarkable – a stable, unvarying, supportive context where the mourner, the bereaved and the broken are lovingly mentored back into life.

Ecstatic spirituality is like romantic love, filling the soul with a burst of light and heat, but soon waning, fading away. It corresponds to the human experience of rebirth and transformation in moments of radical change. The minyan's spirituality bespeaks quiet fidelity and devotion. Like the trusting, deep and loyal affection of the long-married, this spirituality points to the permanent and unchanging in life – all that continues through the trials and crises of life.

The most powerful expression of the minyan's spirituality, and the center of its rite, is the recitation of Kaddish. The Kaddish is not about death. It contains no mention of death. It provides a context in which death can be met and overcome. Kaddish is a reaffirmation of faith in God, the creator and redeemer.

For the one shaken by death, the Kaddish provides a way back to faith, hope and life. Its healing power is not in the radical theology of its words or in extraordinary language of its poetry. Its healing power lies in the simple constancy of its repetition, even in the regularity of the cadences of its syllables: *"Yitgadal 'yitkadash ... yitbarach v'yistabach v'yitpa'ar vyit'nasay ...*"

In his moving book, "Living a Year of Kaddish", Ari Goldman describes the power of Kaddish as an expression of continuity: "To me, the hardest thing about dying must be the not knowing the end of the story. My mother and father left this world while their grandchildren were small. Maybe Kaddish in itself is a kind of afterlife. The one thing my parents know with reasonable certainty was that we, their sons, would be saying Kaddish for them. They would be gone someday, but their Kaddish would live on. I like to think of it as more than a prayer. I think of Kaddish as a portal for the dead to connect to life."

This unique spirituality is born in this week's Torah portion. "The Lord said to Moses: Speak unto the priests, the sons of Aaron, and say to them: 'None [of you] shall defile himself for any [dead] person among his kin, except for the relatives closest to him...'" (Lev 21:1-2) The portion opens with this severe restriction on the service of the priests. It concludes with a detailed description of the priests' responsibilities at each of the yearly festivals and holidays.

The Hasidic master, Mordechai Yosef Leiner, the Ishbitzer Rebbe read the verse as a warning: Confronting death brings tumultuous emotions – rage and bitterness. The Ishbitzer taught that priests serving God are not permitted to touch death, lest they become consumed in the despair and darkness of grief. The priests of ancient Israel offered the daily Tamid and Mincha sacrifices each day. They led the communal rituals sanctifying Sabbaths, New Moons and festivals. But the priest – the agent and embodiment of the community's connection with God – did not officiate at communal rites of grief and mourning. The priest embodied all that was permanent in life, all that continued. He sanctified the rhythms of time, the passing of seasons, the steady movement of the year. Just as the Kaddish does not mention death, priests did not attend funerals. For the priest represents the pathway from death back to life – he holds open the door from darkness back to light, from despair back to hope.

-Rabbi Edward Feinstein

Chapter Five

TIME HEALS

W hen grief is fresh, it is practically impossible to imagine that our feelings will ever change, that we'll ever get used to our loved one's absence from our lives, that we'll ever "get over it." And so often, the rest of the world pushes us to "move on" well before we are ready. "Life is for the living," they say. "It's time to pick up the pieces and go on." Judaism teaches that life is for the living, but the Jewish tradition also provides a structure for healing. As in so many other areas, to do this, Judaism relies upon time. Using time, we can build a different relationship with our absent loved one. We learn that although we will never be "over it," a loved one's passing still allows them to be present to us on a different level and in different ways. We find that we don't even need to "get over" a death; rather, we simply need time to soften grief's sharp edges. As the sources in this chapter suggest, this is a path that each one of us must find and follow; no one can be forced on this journey.

Finding the Way Out of Bagamoyo

You've heard the stories. Cruel slavers in bygone years trek into the African interior and capture men, women and children to sell on the slave market. Then, for weeks upon end, they march their captives to the African coast and force them to board ships bound for the New World.

During those long marches from remote villages, newly acquired slaves were made to carry their captor's heavy loads. Historians report that, at the end of an excruciating day, as evening approached, slavers sometimes shouted to their captives in Swahili, "Bwaga mizigo," which means, "Put down your burdens." Only then could they rest.

When the slaves finally reached the coast, they laid down those burdens for the last time. There they boarded ships that took them away from their loved ones and their homeland forever. Some called that place "Bagamoyo," from the words "bwaga" (put down) and "moyo" (heart). Bagamoyo translates to "Put down your heart." In hopelessness and despair, they put down their hearts and left them on the African continent.

Bagamoyo. I've been there. Haven't you? We've been to our own personal places of despair. Imprisoned by fear and worry and doubts. Trapped by grief. Or betrayed by our own bodies – left to languish in illness and pain. We know how it feels to give up. We know how it feels to desperately wonder if we can go on, or even should go on.

And more than once I've been tempted to lay down my heart and leave it behind. Haven't you? I think we've all been to our own Bagamoyos, those places of deep despair.

But here is the hope. If life teaches me anything, it teaches me that Bagamoyo is a way-point, not a destination. We may each find ourselves there from time to time, but it is not a place to remain. Life cautions that I should never lay my heart down in despair. There is always a way through Bagamoyo.

Author and playwright Jean Kerr put it like this. She said, "Hope is the feeling you have, that the feeling you have, isn't permanent." Hope does not deny the terrible place in which I may find myself. Oh, that's real enough. But it reminds me that Bagamoyo is a only a temporary place. It may seem like a place I'll never leave, but I will. And sometimes it's just enough to know that.

So I've learned to believe in tomorrow. When I believe in tomorrow I can pick up my heart today. When I believe in tomorrow, I can find my way out of Bagamoyo.

And when I do, I'll find my way to life.

-Steve Goodier

Celebrating My Scars

Po Bronson, in his book "Why Do I Love These People?" tells a true story about a scarred and stately elm tree. The tree was planted in the first half of the 20th Century on a farm near Beulah, Michigan (USA). It grew to be magnificent. Today the elm spans some 60 feet across its lush, green crown. Its trunk measures about 12 feet in circumference. And a vivid scar encircles the tree.

In the 1950s the family that owned the farm kept a bull chained to the elm. The bull paced round and round the tree. The heavy iron chain scraped a trench in the bark about three feet off the ground. The trench deepened over the years threatening to kill the tree. But though damaged so severely, the tree strangely did not die.

After some years the family sold the farm and took their bull. They cut the chain, leaving the loop embedded in the trunk and one link hanging down. The elm continued to grow and bark slowly covered parts of the rusting chain that strangled it. The deep gash around the trunk became an ugly scar.

Then one year agricultural catastrophe struck Michigan – in the form of Dutch Elm Disease. A path of death spread across vast areas of countryside. Most elm trees in the vicinity of the farm became infected and died. But that one noble elm remained untouched.

Amazingly, it had survived two hardships. It was not killed by the bull's chain years earlier, and this time it out-lasted the deadly fungus. Year after year it thrived. Nobody could understand why it was still standing in a vast area where most every other elm tree was gone.

Plant pathologists from Michigan State University came out to study the tree. They looked closely at the chain necklace buried deep in the scar. These experts reported that the chain itself actually saved the elm's life. They reasoned that the tree absorbed so much iron from the chain left to rust around its trunk that it became immune to the fungus. What certainly could have killed the tree actually made it stronger and more resilient.

As Ernest Hemingway said, "The world breaks everyone and afterward many are strong at the broken places." The same chain that severely wounded the tree saved its life in the end.

The story of this tree reminds me that the very things that have hurt me, physically as well as emotionally, have also helped me more than I may ever know. Many of them left scars – some of the scars are visible and some not. But these days I am learning to accept my scars – even to celebrate them.

Why not? My scars remind me that I did indeed survive my deepest wounds. That in itself is an accomplishment. And they bring to mind something else, too. They remind me that the damage life has inflicted on me has, in many places, left me stronger and more resilient. What hurt me in the past has actually made me better equipped to face the present.

Yes, I have scars. I have decided to look on them as things of beauty. And I will celebrate them.

-Steve Goodier

Yizkor

If life inexorably ends in death, what is the meaning of life? If before being born we are nothing, and if death returns us to nothing, what is life, what is man? At this sacred time–when children remember parents who have died, when parents remember children that death has snatched from them, when we remember our partners–the question that shakes our souls is: What is life? What is memory? What is forgetfulness? At this sacred time, our conscience will not allow self-deception, even though the truth cannot be uncovered. The question is: What is life when confronted with death? What is memory when confronted with forgetfulness?

Yizkor Eloheinu – May God remember; Remember what we have forgotten. Remember, because forgetfulness is as unavoidable as death. *Yizkor* is a prayer that pleads with God to rescue, from the abyss of forgetfulness, those precious moments of memory that have become buried under decades of shopping visits and work deadlines. Is lightning from a night's storm able to illuminate the night?

Yizkor Eloheinu, May God remember; Remember the lives of the dead, because we who continue to live frequently remember only their deaths, letting their lives be extinguished in forgetfulness. We cry for their deaths; but we cry, even more, for being orphaned, for our emptiness, and our pain.

There is a Chasidic teaching, frequently quoted by Abraham Joshua Heschel, which describes three levels of bereavement.

The first level is tears (the simplest, most general way we express grief).

The second, slightly better level is silence.

The third way, which this Jewish teaching suggests is the highest level of expressing grief, is through song. Crying is our pain, silence our courage, but song is our life. Those who made our lives possible, and filled them with meaning, receive our praises through song.

It is not possible to conquer death, nor to resist forgetfulness. Whoever attempts to do so, resisting forgetfulness and struggling to remember the dead, ends up forgetting the living.

Yizkor Eloheinu – May God remember. God remembers because I must forget, because I am not able to remember, because I need to forget in order to live. Song is the purest way to bear the burden of our bereavement because it makes of all of life a single memory.

Autumn prevails by stripping the trees of all of their leaves, but is defeated, in spite of the storms, because the buds of Spring first appear where Autumn left its victims scattered.

-*Rabbi Marshall T. Meyer*

Take Your Time

Recently I went on a short vacation with my family. Summoning all my resolution for five days, I did not check my email. When I returned I discovered something remarkable.

Of the several hundred messages awaiting me, many were junk, some were important, and a large number had taken care of themselves. Had I checked them right away, answers would have been required, but time took care of the issue. As Emerson wrote in his essay on Napoleon: "He directed Bourrienne to leave all letters unopened for three weeks, and then observed with satisfaction how large a part of the correspondence had thus disposed of itself, and no longer required an answer."

We are slaves to the instant. We respond immediately, giving nothing time to brew, to baste, to boil away. Learning about the world by reading a newspaper, insisted Ben Hecht, was like learning the time by only consulting a second hand. What then of those who learn from the Internet alone? We see each thread, but with our noses pressed close, the tapestry is inaccessible to us. Study, depth, reflection can offer more than the constant point and click that characterize our days.

The Psalmist writes of God: "A thousand years in Your sight are like a day" (Ps 90:4). God sees under the aspect of eternity. Too often in modern times we see things under the aspect of the instant. That which is urgent is not always important; a little distance, a deep breath and a bit of faith can help us distinguish between the two.

-Rabbi David Wolpe

This Too Will Pass

A fable: There was a king who had the most magnificent collection of jewels. This collection was his greatest joy. One night, he dreamed of a ring with special power: When a person was sad, the ring could make him happy; when he was giddy, it sobered him; and when he was joyful, it intensified and heightened his joy. The king awoke convinced that somewhere in the world there was such a ring. He summoned his ministers, described the dream and offered a fabulous reward for the one who found it.

Each of the ministers went out to search and each returned empty-handed, except for one, whose love for his king pushed him onward. For years, he scoured the world, searching to no avail. Finally, he returned home. But before he would confess failure to his king, the minister stopped at a shop near the palace. He described to the jeweler all his trials. The old jeweler simply smiled. "I have the ring." Refusing all payment, he handed an old box to the astonished minister. "Your king needs this ring. Take it as my gift."

The minister rushed to the palace. He entered the king's chamber, approached the throne, and presented his treasure. Opening the box, the king found a plain, unadorned, metal ring with three Hebrew words engraved upon it:

Gam Zeh Ya-Avor – This Too Will Pass.

The king soon realized the magical power of the ring. When he was sad, the ring reminded him: *This Too Will Pass,* and he was consoled. When he was senseless, he looked upon the ring, *This Too Will Pass,* and returned to himself. And when he experienced true joy, the ring reminded him: *This Too Will*

Pass, and he learned to hold and cherish precious moments. All his many jewels paled in the face of the plain metal ring which never left his hand.

The story is true. The ring and its magic really exist. It is the greatest magic of all: Learning to live with the passage of time. This is the wisdom of the magic ring. This is the wisdom of Yizkor. We learn that those who fight time are destined to lose. No one lives forever. We learn that those who ignore time, or neglect time, or kill time, lose the poignancy, the intensity, the gifts of life. They let life slip away. Four times a year, we come to Yizkor to learn to live with time.

It is said, "Time heals all wounds." This is true...but only for the minor wounds. The rude waiter, the traffic jam, the broken appliance are forgotten with the passage of time. The irritations and aggravations of life fade with time. But the real pain – the painful loss of those we love, the loneliness after they are gone – never goes away. Over time, the sweetness of memory comes to leaven the bitterness of loss. The pain, the loneliness is still there. But it mellows as it is displaced by our profound gratitude for their lives, for the precious moments we shared. *This Too Will Pass*.

When we are lighthearted – giddy, and tipsy...when life becomes a constant search for distraction, for amusement, for entertainment...we remember, *This Too Will Pass*. No one has an endless supply of tomorrows to accomplish the important tasks of life. What's important in life? What's real in life? And if not now, when?

And when we are truly happy...As we sit at a Seder table with children and grandchildren, with friends of a lifetime ... we also remember *This Too Will Pass*. Children grow older and move away. Loved ones pass on. We remember that these moments of joy are fleeting. They come and go so quickly. We must pay attention; hold onto these moments and cherish them. The bitterness of mortality teaches us mindfulness for the moments that matter.

In the movie Avalon, the filmmaker Barry Levinson, pictures his family at the Thanksgiving (or the Pesach Seder) table, sitting together, sharing life's joys and struggles. Then one year, a slight – the turkey was cut before someone arrived – and that was the last Thanksgiving together: From then on, only bitter acrimony, "You cut the turkey!" Never again would the family sit together; never again, until death brought them to graveside to learn the bitter lesson.

Is there a family among us without such bitterness? We are angry. We hold grudges. We remember insults. And we never forgive. We never let go, until one day someone dies. And then, suddenly, we remember the ring's wisdom, but tragically, because at graveside it is too late. At graveside we can only cry for all the years wasted, all the love squandered, all the precious moments neglected. Do we think we have each other forever? Have we learned nothing from Yizkor?

There is a puzzling ceremony in the Passover Seder. Just before we eat the meal, comes *Korech* – the "Hillel sandwich." Hillel, the first century sage, combined all the sacred foods of the Seder in one bite – the Passover sacrifice, the matza, the *marror,* the *charoset*. In *Korech*, we taste something special. Eating the biting, bitter *marror* and the sweet *charoset* all together, we savor the taste of life – and the taste of life is bittersweet. Bittersweet. The *charoset* mellows the sting of the *marror* and makes it digestible. The *marror* brings out the sweetness of the *charoset*. Bittersweet is life lived in full awareness of the passage of time.

Those whose lives have never been touched by death don't understand. They expect life to be all happiness. They are so deeply disappointed when it isn't. They turn cynical and depressive and dwell upon the darkness. But those who have learned how to live in time – how to wear the king's magic ring – learn to savor the bittersweet taste of life, mellowing the choking bitterness of mortality with the passion of precious sweet moments.

-*Rabbi Edward Feinstein*

Bittersweet

The classical explanation for breaking a glass at the end of the wedding is to recall the destruction of Jerusalem. As the glass is broken, everyone screams out *Mazel Tov*! There is something peculiar, not only about recalling an historic tragedy at that exact moment, but also shouting for joy just as it is recalled.

Yet the message is the same as bitter herbs on Passover. We do not only eat bitter herbs, we make a blessing over them. Then we dip them into *haroset*, which is sweet. The duality of life is symbolized by the historical memory wrapped in a wedding, and the bitter herb mixed with the *haroset*. Bitterness is not incidental and not fleeting but it is also not final. In defiance of hundreds of years of slavery (bitter herbs) or national catastrophe (the broken glass) we affirm the essential goodness of life that can be so painful.

It is tricky to be optimistic without being simultaneously in denial. Judaism manages the delicate balancing act: pain is real, even at our most celebratory moments. But final victory belongs to the sweetness, the embrace, the promise that one day all weeping will give way to joy.

-Rabbi David Wolpe

Chapter Six

ROSEBUDS: WHEN A CHILD DIES

Whenever the Sages of the Talmud were confronted by some theory of perfect earthly justice, their response was always the same. Children die. Can there be anything more unfair, more unjust than this? One Sage's tale of reward for doing *mitzvot*, the commandments of Jewish law, is met by another's account of a child dying while doing as God has commanded. In one such incident, the Sage Elisha ben Abuya witnessed a child fall to his death from a tree while sending away a mother bird to gather eggs, as the Torah commands. His immediate response: "There is no justice, and no Judge." He found the very existence of God to be incompatible with this bitterest reality, that children die.

Rabbi Elliot J. Cosgrove, in a 2014 Yom Kippur sermon centered upon Rabbi Milton Steinberg's work about Elisha ben Abuya, "As A Driven Leaf", suggested, if not a solution, at least a path to follow. He noted that Elisha ben Abuya's response to God's apparent lack of care for the world was to leave his community. Rabbi Cosgrove recounts a final meeting between Elisha ben Abuya and his student, Rabbi Meir, during which Rabbi Meir sees forgiveness even for the affirmed apostate ben Abuya:

"Only this year did it finally dawn on me that the voice of Rabbi Meir calling on Elisha to return was the voice of Rabbi Steinberg calling his Jews back into the communal fold. 'Turn back,' Meir cried, even now, with all your doubts, you can return. Rabbi Meir made no claim to have the answers to Elisha's questions. If anything, having buried two of his own children, he experienced those questions weighing more heavily on his soul than they did on that of his teacher. But what Rabbi Meir knew was that although he lacked the answers, there was still comfort, solace, and support to be found in community."

Rabbi Cosgrove points out that theology and philosophy

are no help here. We, however, are the best source of help for each other.

How The Innocent Have Fallen!

How the innocent have fallen!
Beloved and pleasant in life
Undivided in death.

How the innocent have fallen!
Who haven't yet lived.
Their families, their friends
Prayed for them
But their words fell on deaf ears
Like stones.
Woe to them, and us.

How the innocent have fallen!
By cruel men of terror.
Whence will comfort come
To parents and cousins,
To friends and our nation weeping
Streams of water for the loss?

How the innocent have fallen!
Not yet tasting
Sweet life.
Garden of Eden be their stop
Until they rise again
Giving life to the dead.

-Rabbi Gerald B. Weiss

When the Good Die Young

The teachings of reincarnation are of value when we have nowhere else to turn in the tragedy of a death. Whether it is the death of a young child or of a young adult in his or her prime, sometimes we can find solace in understanding that the task they came to do was completed and they had to move on. Indeed, there is a teaching that says, "The good die early so that they do not risk being corrupted, and the wicked live longer so that they have more chance to repent." [Zohar I:56b]

-Rabbi David A. Cooper

Dvir

Dvir Aminolav was the first Israeli soldier killed in the 2008 Gaza War. His mother Dalya missed Dvir, terribly. One night before she went to bed, she said in a loud voice: "G-d, give me a sign, give me a hug from Dvir so that I will know that his death had some meaning."

That week her daughter asked her to accompany her to a musical performance at The International Crafts Festival in Jerusalem. Dalya, feeling quite depressed, did not want to go to the concert, but she didn't want to disappoint her daughter either, and agreed to go halfheartedly. The concert was a bit delayed. A two-year-old boy began wandering through the stands. He walked up to Dalya's seat and touched her on the shoulder. A preschool teacher, Dalya turned around, saw the boy and smiled warmly.

"What's your name?" Dalya asked.

"Eshel," the boy replied.

"That's a nice name. Do you want to be my friend, Eshel?" The boy nodded in reply and sat down next to Dalya.

Eshel's parents were sitting two rows above. Concerned their son was bothering Dalya, they asked him to come back up. But Dalya insisted that everything was fine.

"I have a brother named Dvir," two-year-old Eshel chimed in, as only little children can. Dalya was shocked to hear the unusual name of her beloved son, and walked up the two rows to where Eshel's parents were sitting. She saw a baby in his carriage, and apologizing, she asked, "If you don't mind me asking, how old is your baby and when was he born?"

The baby's mother replied, "He was born right after the war in Gaza."

Dalya swallowed hard. "Please tell me, why did you choose to name him Dvir?"

Baby Dvir's mother began to explain. "When I was at the end of my pregnancy, the doctors suspected the fetus may have a very serious birth defect. Since it was the end of the pregnancy, there was little the doctors could do and I just had to wait and see how things would turn out. When I went home that night, the news reported that the first casualty in the war was a soldier named Dvir. I was so saddened by this news that I decided to make a deal with G-d. 'If you give me a healthy son,' I said in my prayer, 'I promise to name him Dvir, in memory of the soldier that was killed.'"

Dalya, the mother of Dvir, stood with her mouth open. She tried to speak but she couldn't. After a long silence, she said quietly, "I am Dvir's mother."

The young parents didn't believe her. She repeated, "Yes, it's true. I am Dvir's mother. My name is Dalya Aminalov, from Pisgat Ze'ev."

With a sudden inspiration, Baby Dvir's mother handed Dalya the baby and said, "Dvir wants to give you a hug."

Dalya held the little baby boy in her arms and looked into his angelic face. The emotion she felt at that moment was overwhelming. She had asked for a hug from Dvir – and she could truly feel his warm and loving embrace.

Living for their Dreams

Rabbi Harold Kushner, in his beautiful meditation on the Twenty-Third Psalm, The Lord Is My Shepherd, has some wise advice for us in regard to dealing with loss. Being one of the world's authorities on this subject, and having had his own terrible tragedy in his life – the loss of his teenage son to a rare disease – his ideas are always worth taking seriously.

He suggests that one way to honor the memory of our loved ones who have passed on, is to continue to live the kind of life that they would have wanted us to live. When he speaks to groups of bereaved parents (since he is one, he does this often), he reminds them that they have inherited their child's unlived years. And that part of that inheritance is to do the things their children never lived to do. Instead of saying that their lives are finished, that they will never get over this loss, they might try to find ways to live out the dreams, ideals, aspirations, their child would have wanted to fulfill.

Rabbi Kushner asks those he counsels, "Had you been the

one to die first, what advice would you have left for your loved ones? How would you have wanted him/her to spend the rest of his/her life?"

When the mourner replies that they would have advised their spouse to go on living as full a life as possible, as a tribute to the shared life of the couple, he then tells them to try to do the same thing, and take their own advice.

For this reason, he explains, the Jewish tradition gives us four opportunities a year to remember those whom we have loved and lost – during Yizkor time. Yizkor gives us permission, he claims, to go on with our lives without worrying that we may have forgotten the painful and sacred memories they cherish.

"I urge people," he concludes, "to see that the same love that makes the death of a person hurt so much is the love that should inspire us to keep walking through the valley, in tribute to the power and holiness of life even in the face of death."

-D.P.E.

Redeeming Suffering With Presence

In the Talmud, the death of a child is taken as proof that there is such a thing as meaningless, irredeemable suffering. Whenever one rabbi tries to see meaning in suffering, some hidden benefit or a course correction when we've gone astray, another rabbi will bring up the death of a child, which the Talmud takes as an unassailable refutation that suffering could have any meaning at all.

Suffering is just suffering. According to Buddhists, suffering is the first noble truth, and it is relentless. We can never escape it or explain it away. I never understood this so thoroughly as when I was working on the pediatric ward at Sloan Kettering. I never felt the impulse to run away from suffering as strongly as I felt it there. In the end, I didn't run away. In the end, I sat by the bedsides of these children and in the waiting room with their parents. I sat until I got past seeing my own children and their vulnerability in these children. I sat until I realized the great truth that Rabbi Yochanan came to at the end of the Talmudic discussion on suffering: Our attempts to understand suffering and to give it meaning are futile and empty, and the death of children proves it. Suffering is an irreducible and inevitable mystery and can only be met by a mystery of equal force – the power of simple human presence to heal. Rabbi Yochanan sat with the dying, young and old, tried to explain their suffering to them, and when he failed to do so, he simply sat with them in silence, held their hands, wept with them, and that seemed to work, that brought healing. So I sat with these children and their families day after day, praying that Rabbi Yochanan was right.

-Rabbi Alan Lew

Loving Life More, Being More Aware

Death always brings one suddenly face to face with life. Nothing, not even the birth of one's child, brings one so close to life as his death.

During Johnny's illness, I prayed continually to God, naturally, God was always there. He sat beside us during the doctors' consultation, as we waited the long vigils outside the operating room, as we rejoiced in the miracle of a brief recovery, as we agonized when hope ebbed away and the doctors confessed there was no longer anything they could do. They were helpless, and we were helpless, and in His way, God, standing by us in our hour of need, God, in His infinite wisdom and mercy and loving kindness, God in all His omnipotence, was helpless too.

I wish we had loved Johnny more when he was alive. Of course we loved Johnny very much. Johnny knew that. Everybody knew it. Loving Johnny more. What does it mean? What can it mean now?

Parents all over the earth who lost sons in the war have felt this kind of question, and sought an answer.

To me, it means loving life more, being more aware of life, of one's fellow human beings, of the earth.

It means obliterating, in a curious but real way, the ideas of evil and hate and the enemy, and transmuting them, with the alchemy of suffering, into ideas of clarity and charity.

It means caring more and more about other people, at home and abroad, all over the earth. It means caring more about God.

I hope we can love Johnny more and more till we, too, die, and leave behind us, as he did the love of love, the love of life.

-Frances Gunther

Leiby

A few days short of his ninth birthday, Leiby Kletzky was abducted and murdered on his way home from a Brooklyn day camp.

A Hasidic legend teaches us, that each time we pray, we create a new angel. Nine-year-old Leiby asked his Rebbe, "How do we know we are creating a good angel? Maybe the angel will have negative traits."

The Rebbe replied, "Leiby, if you pray with true *kavanah*, you will be creating the good angels." Leiby, during the few years given to him, brought much sweetness into our often bitter world.

-Unknown

Chapter Seven

FALLEN HEROES

Who is a hero? The answer might seem simple: soldiers, police officers, fire fighters, first responders to emergencies and disasters. And indeed, every year some of these give their lives in the line of duty, and we all recognize that they are heroes. This chapter concentrates on them, because of the special circumstances in which they too often meet their deaths. They act without thought for their own safety; they give their lives in the service of others, in the service of their country, for causes like freedom that they see as larger than themselves.

Others too can be heroes. Perhaps the newspapers don't report their bravery; perhaps only those closest to them know of it. Whenever we think of someone and hope to emulate their selflessness, their courage, their dedication and devotion, we have found a hero, whether in life or death.

The Gettysburg Address

The Gettysburg National Cemetery was dedicated by President Abraham Lincoln just four months after the Civil War's Battle of Gettysburg, which claimed nearly 8,000 lives. Lincoln's two-minute speech followed the main oration of the day, which lasted some two hours, but it is Lincoln's brief remarks that we remember as the Gettysburg Address.

> Four score and seven years ago, our fathers brought forth on this continent a new nation: conceived in liberty, and dedicated to the proposition that all men are created equal.
>
> Now we are engaged in a great civil war ... testing whether that nation, or any nation so conceived and so dedicated ... can long endure. We are met on a great battlefield of that war.

We have come to dedicate a portion of that field as a final resting place for those who here gave their lives that that nation might live. It is altogether fitting and proper that we should do this.

But, in a larger sense, we cannot dedicate ... we cannot consecrate ... we cannot hallow this ground. The brave men, living and dead, who struggled here have consecrated it, far above our poor power to add or detract. The world will little note, nor long remember, what we say here, but it can never forget what they did here. It is for us the living, rather, to be dedicated here to the unfinished work which they who fought here have thus far so nobly advanced.

It is rather for us to be here dedicated to the great task remaining before us ... that from these honored dead we take increased devotion to that cause for which they gave the last full measure of devotion ... that we here highly resolve that these dead shall not have died in vain ... that this nation, under God, shall have a new birth of freedom ... and that government of the people ... by the people ... for the people ... shall not perish from the earth.

-Abraham Lincoln

The Young Dead Soldiers Do Not Speak

The young dead soldiers do not speak.

Nevertheless, they are heard in the still houses:
who has not heard them?

They have a silence that speaks for them at night
and when the clock counts.

They say: We were young. We have died.
Remember us.

They say: We have done what we could
but until it is finished it is not done.

They say: We have given our lives but until it is finished
no one can know what our lives gave.

They say: Our deaths are not ours: they are yours,
they will mean what you make them.

They say: Whether our lives and our deaths were for
peace and a new hope or for nothing we cannot say,
it is you who must say this.

We leave you our deaths. Give them their meaning.
We were young, they say. We have died; remember us.

-Archibald MacLeish

High Flight

Oh, I have slipped the surly bonds of Earth,
And danced the skies on laughter-silvered wings;
Sunward I've climbed, and joined the tumbling mirth
Of sun-split clouds – and done a hundred things you have
    not dreamed of – wheeled and soared and swung high
    in the sunlit silence.
Hovering there I've chased the shouting wind along
    and flung my eager craft through footless halls of air.
Up, up the long delirious, burning blue
I've topped the windswept heights with easy grace,
    where never lark or even eagle flew;
    and, while with silent lifting mind I've trod
    the high untrespassed sanctity of space,
    put out my hand and touched the face of God.

- by Pilot Officer John Gillespie Magee Junior.
No 412 Squadron RCAF, killed on December 11, 1941.

("High Flight" became known to another generation when
President Ronald Reagan, in a speech written by Peggy Noonan,
quoted from the poem in his eulogy for the seven astronauts of
the Challenger, killed when the space shuttle exploded during
launch on January 28, 1986.)

A Lesson from the Titanic – Love Flows Continuously

This is the year of the Titanic and our celebration of a tragedy. A grocery buyer from Macy's, John A. Badenoch, had been traveling to Europe and was on the rescue ship, the Carpathia. He knew that the Strauses were on the Titanic and he gathered stories from survivors, trying to piece together what happened to the couple. He wrote to the Straus children that their parents showed courage and composure to the end. The following is the account relayed in his letter:

"Mr. And Mrs. Straus were in bed at the time of the accident ... Shortly thereafter, they appeared on the deck, fully clothed, mingled with the other passengers and discussed the danger in a perfectly calm and collected manner.

"They evidently did not believe that there was any great danger of the ship sinking. On the advice of the captain, they put on a life preserver over their fur coats and assisted other passengers in doing the same. By that time, the boats were being filled with women and children, and your mother was asked by the officer in charge and urged by your father to get into one of the lifeboats. She refused to do so and insisted that the maid take her place in boat number 8.

"Finally, when it became apparent that there was no hope of the Titanic staying afloat, your father insisted that your mother enter the second from the last boat that was being launched from the side they were on. She still refused, saying she would not go without him ... an officer in charge again urged her to enter and, in fact, attempted force, aided by the urging of your father. She placed her foot in the boat, thinking at the time that your father would accompany her.

"Mr. Isidor, thinking that your mother was safe in the lifeboat, stepped back with the other men. Your mother, looking around and seeing your father was not with her, got out of the boat, went to where your father was standing and put her arms around him. The officer in charge, seeing that it was no use in trying to get your mother to leave your father, ordered the boat lowered away.

"She was quoted as saying, 'We have been living together for many years, and wherever you go, I do.' "

A Straus family mausoleum was erected in Woodlawn Cemetery in the Bronx. The stone contains Isidor's and Ida's date of birth and death. An inscription from the Bible reads: "Many waters cannot quench love – neither can the floods destroy."

The Straus's understood the love that flows continuously from bonds nurtured by their faith; in death, they affirmed that faith.

-D.P.E.

I Think Continually Of Those Who Were Truly Great

I think continually of those who were truly great.
Who, from the womb, remembered the soul's history
Through corridors of light where the hours are suns
Endless and singing. Whose lovely ambition
Was that their lips, still touched with fire,
Should tell of the Spirit clothed from head to foot in song.
And who hoarded from the Spring branches
The desires falling across their bodies like blossoms.

What is precious is never to forget
The essential delight of the blood drawn from ageless springs
Breaking through rocks in worlds before our earth.
Never to deny its pleasure in the morning simple light
Nor its grave evening demand for love.
Never to allow gradually the traffic to smother
With noise and fog the flowering of the spirit.

Near the snow, near the sun, in the highest fields
See how these names are feted by the waving grass
And by the streamers of white cloud
And whispers of wind in the listening sky.
The names of those who in their lives fought for life
Who wore at their hearts the fire's center.
Born of the sun they traveled a short while towards the sun,
And left the vivid air signed with their honor.

-Stephen Spender

President Obama's Remarks in Tucson

Following is a text of President Obama's prepared address on Wednesday, January 12, 2011, to honor those killed and wounded in a shooting on January 8, 2011, as released by the White House.

To the families of those we've lost; to all who called them friends; to the students of this university, the public servants gathered tonight, and the people of Tucson and Arizona: I have come here tonight as an American who, like all Americans, kneels to pray with you today, and will stand by you tomorrow.

There is nothing I can say that will fill the sudden hole torn in your hearts. But know this: the hopes of a nation are here tonight. We mourn with you for the fallen. We join you in your grief. And we add our faith to yours that Representative Gabrielle Giffords and the other living victims of this tragedy pull through.

As Scripture tells us: There is a river whose streams make glad the city of God, the holy place where the Most High dwells. God is within her, she will not fall; God will help her at break of day.

On Saturday morning, Gabby, her staff, and many of her constituents gathered outside a supermarket to exercise their right to peaceful assembly and free speech. They were fulfilling a central tenet of the democracy envisioned by our founders – representatives of the people answering to their constituents, so as to carry their concerns to our nation's capital. Gabby called it "Congress on Your Corner" – just an updated version of government of and by and for the people.

That is the quintessentially American scene that was shattered by a gunman's bullets. And the six people who lost their lives on Saturday – they too represented what is best in America.

Our hearts are broken by their sudden passing. Our hearts are broken – and yet, our hearts also have reason for fullness.

These men and women remind us that heroism is found not only on the fields of battle. They remind us that heroism does not require special training or physical strength. Heroism is here, all around us, in the hearts of so many of our fellow citizens, just waiting to be summoned – as it was on Saturday morning.

Their actions, their selflessness, also pose a challenge to each of us. It raises the question of what, beyond the prayers and expressions of concern, is required of us going forward. How can we honor the fallen? How can we be true to their memory?

You see, when a tragedy like this strikes, it is part of our nature to demand explanations – to try to impose some order on the chaos, and make sense out of that which seems senseless. Already we've seen a national conversation commence, not only about the motivations behind these killings, but about everything from the merits of gun safety laws to the adequacy of our mental health systems. Much of this process, of debating what might be done to prevent such tragedies in the future, is an essential ingredient in our exercise of self-government.

But at a time when our discourse has become so sharply polarized – at a time when we are far too eager to lay the blame for all that ails the world at the feet of those who think differently than we do – it's important for us to pause for a moment and make sure that we are talking with each other in a way that heals, not a way that wounds.

Scripture tells us that there is evil in the world, and that terrible things happen for reasons that defy human understanding. In the words of Job, "when I looked for light, then came darkness." Bad things happen, and we must guard against simple explanations in the aftermath.

For the truth is that none of us can know exactly what triggered this vicious attack. None of us can know with any certainty what might have stopped those shots from being fired, or what thoughts lurked in the inner recesses of a violent man's mind.

So yes, we must examine all the facts behind this tragedy. We cannot and will not be passive in the face of such violence. We should be willing to challenge old assumptions in order to lessen the prospects of violence in the future.

But what we can't do is use this tragedy as one more occasion to turn on one another. As we discuss these issues, let each of us do so with a good dose of humility. Rather than pointing fingers or assigning blame, let us use this occasion to expand our moral imaginations, to listen to each other more carefully, to sharpen our instincts for empathy, and remind ourselves of all the ways our hopes and dreams are bound together.

After all, that's what most of us do when we lose someone in our family – especially if the loss is unexpected. We're shaken from our routines, and forced to look inward. We reflect on the past. Did we spend enough time with an aging parent, we wonder. Did we express our gratitude for all the sacrifices they made for us? Did we tell a spouse just how desperately we loved them, not just once in awhile but every single day?

So sudden loss causes us to look backward – but it also forces us to look forward, to reflect on the present and the future, on the manner in which we live our lives and nurture our relationships with those who are still with us. We may ask ourselves if we've shown enough kindness and generosity and compassion to the people in our lives.

Perhaps we question whether we are doing right by our children, or our community, and whether our priorities are in order. We recognize our own mortality, and are reminded that in the fleeting time we have on this earth, what matters is not wealth, or status, or power, or fame – but rather, how well we have loved, and what small part we have played in bettering the lives of others.

That process of reflection, of making sure we align our values with our actions – that, I believe, is what a tragedy like this requires. For those who were harmed, those who were killed – they are part of our family, an American family 300 million strong. We may not have known them personally, but we surely see ourselves in them. In George and Dot, in Dorwan and Mavy, we sense the abiding love we have for our own husbands, our own wives, our own life partners. Phyllis – she's our mom or grandma; Gabe our brother or son. In Judge Roll, we recognize not only a man who prized his family and doing his job well, but also a man who embodied America's fidelity to the law. In Gabby, we see a reflection of our public spiritedness, that desire to participate in that sometimes frustrating, sometimes contentious, but always necessary and never-ending process to form a more perfect union.

And in Christina ... in Christina we see all of our children. So curious, so trusting, so energetic and full of magic.

So deserving of our love. And so deserving of our good example. If this tragedy prompts reflection and debate, as it should, let's make sure it's worthy of those we have lost. Let's make sure it's not on the usual plane of politics and point scoring and pettiness that drifts away with the next news cycle. The loss of these wonderful people should make every one of us strive to be better in our private lives – to be better friends and neighbors, co-workers and parents. And if, as has been discussed in recent days, their deaths help usher in more civility in our public discourse, let's remember that it is not because a simple lack of civility caused this tragedy, but rather because only a more civil and honest public discourse can help us face up to our challenges as a nation, in a way that would make them proud. It should be because we want to live up to the example of public servants like John Roll and Gabby Giffords, who knew first and foremost that we are all Americans, and that we can question each other's ideas without questioning each other's love of country, and that our task, working together, is to constantly widen the circle of our concern so that we bequeath the American dream to future generations.

I believe we can be better. Those who died here, those who saved lives here – they help me believe. We may not be able to stop all evil in the world, but I know that how we treat one another is entirely up to us. I believe that for all our imperfections, we are full of decency and goodness, and that the forces that divide us are not as strong as those that unite us.

That's what I believe, in part because that's what a child like Christina Taylor Green believed. Imagine: here was a young girl who was just becoming aware of our democracy; just beginning to understand the obligations of citizenship; just starting to glimpse the fact that someday she too might play a part in shaping her nation's future. She had been elected to her student council; she saw public service as something exciting, something hopeful. She was off to meet her congresswoman, someone she was sure was good and important and might be a role model. She saw all this through the eyes of a child, undimmed by the cynicism or vitriol that we adults all too often just take for granted.

I want us to live up to her expectations. I want our democracy to be as good as she imagined it. All of us – we should do everything we can to make sure this country lives up to our children's expectations.

Christina was given to us on September 11th, 2001, one of 50 babies born that day to be pictured in a book called "Faces of Hope." On either side of her photo in that book were simple wishes for a child's life. "I hope you help those in need," read one. "I hope you know all of the words to the National Anthem and sing it with your hand over your heart. I hope you jump in rain puddles."

If there are rain puddles in heaven, Christina is jumping in them today. And here on Earth, we place our hands over our hearts, and commit ourselves as Americans to forging a country that is forever worthy of her gentle, happy spirit.

May God bless and keep those we've lost in restful and eternal peace. May He love and watch over the survivors. And may He bless the United States of America.

One Who Lost His Life At War

Only those are fit to live who do not fear to die; and none are fit to die who have shrunk from the joy of life and the duty of life. Both life and death are parts of the same Great Adventure.

Unless men are willing to fight and die for great ideals, including love of country, ideals will vanish, and the world will be one huge sty of materialism … All of us who give service, and stand ready for sacrifice, are the torchbearers … The torches whose flames are brightest are borne by the gallant men at the front. These are the torchbearers; these are they who have dared the Great Adventure.

-Theodore Roosevelt

Chapter Eight

NUMBERING OUR DAYS ARIGHT: LESSONS FOR THE LIVING

In the face of death, how do we give life meaning? How do we find ways to move through our lives with our heads up, with no regrets? Each of us has (or must seek) our own answer to this dilemma. We each face different challenges; we each have different examples before us. But it is part of our nature as humans in the image of God to seek meaning in life, and an affirmation that the act of living is meaningful. We are called to find perspective even in the midst of pain. It is this drive that pulls us ahead as we cope with loss and grief.

Teach Us To Number Our Days

If you had a bank that credited your account each morning with $86,400 and carried over no balance from day to day, and allowed you to keep no cash in your account, and every evening canceled whatever part of the amount you had failed to use during the day, what would you do? Draw out every cent, of course.

Well, you have such a bank account, and its name is "Time." Every morning it credits you with 86,400 seconds. Every night it rules off, as lost, whatever of this you have failed to invest to good purpose. It carries over no balances. It allows no overdrafts. Invest it wisely!

-Anonymous – Psalm 90:12

Teach Us To Number Our Days, That We May Achieve a Wise Heart

Using our time wisely is one of the most effective ways to honor our beloved departed.

According to an old fable, the devils were assembled at a

convention. Their theme – how to do their work more effectively. One said, "When I want to get my work done, I convince people that there is no God." People then do everything I want them to do. They are not accountable, they're not responsible.

The second one said: "I do it a little differently. I say to them 'You can believe in God, but you don't have to follow all the laws and commandments. The Bible is not true. So you're on your own.' When he's on his own, he's doing my thing. "

The third devil said: "I don't use either of these devices. I tell them there is a God and the Bible is true. But what's your hurry? You've got plenty of time! "

-Rabbi Hillel E. Silverman

Judaism's Advice For a Meaningful Life

Some of the great religions of the East propose to teach their members how to avoid pain and heartbreak and their secret is really a very simply one; they can teach you, in two words, how to avoid ever being hurt by life, would you like to know their secret? Don't care!

Don't care about people, and you'll never be hurt if you lose them.

Don't trust anybody, and nobody will ever disappoint you or break your heart. Don't cherish anything, and you'll never be saddened at its being taken from you. Don't love, don't trust, don't cherish, and I guarantee that you will never weep. There are religions, great and venerable ones, that teach that. But Judaism teaches us just the opposite: Care deeply and be prepared to pay the price that loving entails.

Love your parents, though it means someday seeing them grow old and weak, and your hands will be powerless to help them. Love them, though it means that someday you will lose them and feel that a part of you has died with them.

Love your children, though it will cause you so many sleepless nights. Love them, though it means feeling the pain of the scraped knees and their hurt feelings. Love them, though that will only make it harder for you one day to see them grow up and go out on their own. But do it the hard way; love them and trust them enough to let them do that.

It says, love your fellow humans, even though it would be so much easier to be callously indifferent to them. But love them, because to do anything else is to abdicate your humanity. To avoid the pain of being alive. To live means to be sensitive to pain and hurt, in the same way that the living raw flesh is so sensitive to every touch, while the dead cells can be cut and scraped and never feel a thing.

Judaism doesn't teach us how to avoid pain and sorrow; it teaches us how to stand up to it without being broken by it. How to live in a world where painful tragic things happen, and still affirm it to be God's world.

And then there is one more thing that Judaism would offer to do for us, to help us live as people were meant to live. There is a dream each of us has secretly in our heart – unless some of us have already given it up as untenable or unattainable – the ambition to be somebody significant, to matter, to make a difference in the world. None of us wants to feel that, at the end of his days, he will have passed through the world and left no trace behind, that he has had no real impact on the world. We would like to justify our existence, to stake our claim to some sort of immortality, on some remarkable achievement that will leave the world different for our having been part of it. And yet, what can we do? Very few, if any, of us will write a book that will be read twenty years from now. Its not likely that any of us in this room today will come up with a medical discovery that will save lives, or an invention that will enrich lives. Who of us will have a bridge, a street, a building named after him?

But Judaism speaks to this secret yearning of ours, and says that it is possible. It is within the power of everyone of us to be a memorable person, to live a significant and impressive life. Judaism offers us not only the secrets of life, but the secret of immortality, of living beyond our appointed years – How to be the kind of parent who will be remembered with words of blessing, how to be a friend who won't easily be forgotten, how to be the kind of neighbor whose impact on a community will remain even after he is gone from the scene.

Anyone's life can be fashioned into a spiritual masterpiece. The equivalent of sainthood is not reserved for a small group of unusual souls who are separated from the rest of society.

Sainthood, that is, a life of spiritual excellence, is the prerogative of every normal husband or wife, parent, working person, anyone who takes life seriously. You don't have to have a particular talent for religion to be a spiritual remarkable person.

-Rabbi Steven Saltzman

Unetaneh Tokef – **There Is No Tomorrow**

He worked hard all his life.
He promised his family that they would go on a vacation.
He assured his wife that they would have time for themselves.
He told his children that he would take them to the park.
He told himself and his family that he was working like
      a dog for their sake, in order to give them
      the type of life they dreamed of.
Soon the time would come.

But "that time" never came.
Now, as he stood before the Divine court, he cried.
Looking down, he saw a grieving family and
      a heart-broken wife.
He saw a thousand dreams unfulfilled.

And he cried out to God:
"Where is the justice in this?
I worked hard all my life. I was an honest man
      who tried to earn a living.
Why have you robbed me of my precious dreams?
Where is the time I wanted to spend with my family?"

God sighed and said:
"Didn't you know that there is no tomorrow, only today?
No one can know 'who shall live and who shall die.'
No one can know what the coming year will hold."

There is no tomorrow, only today. All we have is this moment
      and how we use it.

Unetaneh Tokef Kedushat Hayom

We acknowledge the powerful sanctity of today
Because we cannot know
What the future will hold.

Therefore let us turn while we can,
Let us live while we can,
Let us reach out while we can,
Let us act while we can.
Let us speak words of prayer, words of kindness
While we can.

Let us live each day as if there were no other.
For this day, every day,
Is endowed with powerful sanctity.

-Rabbi Mark B. Greenspan

U'Tzedakah

[R. Yehudah] used to say:
Ten strong things have been created in the world.
The rock is hard but the iron cleaves it.
The iron is hard, but the fire softens it.
The fire is hard, but the water quenches it.
The water is strong, but the clouds bear it.
The clouds are strong, but the wind scatters them.
The wind is strong, but the body bears it.
The body is strong, but fright crushes it.
Fright is strong, but wine banishes it.
Wine is strong, but sleep works it off.

Death is stronger than all, and charity saves from death, as it is written in Proverbs 10:2, "Tzedakah delivers from death."

-Talmud, Bava Batra 10a

Chasing a Dream

In his book "Asimov Laughs Again", author Isaac Asimov

relates an incident when he was interviewed by television journalist Barbara Walters.

She asked him how many books he had written and then asked, "Don't you ever want to do anything but write?"

He said, "No."

She pressed on. "Don't you want to go hunting? Fishing? Dancing? Hiking?"

This time he answered, "No! No! No! And no!"

She continued, "But what would you do if the doctor gave you only six months to live?"

"Type faster."

Isaac Asimov spent his life doing what he loved. I am aware that there are those people who find no satisfaction or joy from making a living. They don't like what they do and they live for weekends and holidays. Some of them feel trapped and believe they can't make a meaningful change because they don't have the skills, education, money or favorable circumstances. So they decide to dig in and keep on slogging forward.

I don't want to say they are wrong, for there are many reasons we each choose our individual paths. But I'm drawn to a truth expressed so clearly by Norman Cousins. "The tragedy of life is not death," says Cousins, "but what we let die inside of us while we live." I agree. Death is not a tragedy in itself. All of us will die. It is as natural as birth. The tragedy is what we let die inside us while we live. Like unrealized dreams. Like a passion to be or do something that is calling to us from someplace deep. The real tragedy of life is settling for less while something dies inside us.

Leaving the safety of what is known and venturing into the unknown can be one of the scariest – and best – decisions a person can make. "There is no security in following the call to adventure," writer Joseph Campbell says. I know what he is talking about. I've followed that call more than once. And it can be frightening. But you know what's worse? Regret. Looking back and wishing that we had risked the adventure. Or just letting the desire dry up and finally die.

Leaving what feels secure behind and following the beckoning of our hearts doesn't always end as we expect or hope. We may even fail. But here's the payoff: it can also be amazing and wonderful and immensely satisfying.

In the end, we really only have one question when it comes to chasing a significant dream. It is whether we will say yes.

-Steve Goodier

My Mother and Helen Keller

Helen Keller, deaf and blind, who managed to teach and write and educate a generation, told us: "The world is full of suffering but also full of the overcoming of it." All around us each day are people struggling with disease, infirmity, loneliness, hunger, and the possible loss of hope. Yet many of those same people are paragons of goodness, of giving, and of love. It does not erase the obstacles in life, but each day they arise anew knowing that the world requires "the overcoming of it."

Visiting my mother recently in Philadelphia I saw a woman who for over 25 years following a cerebral hemorrhage, has been aphasic, almost completely unable to speak, confined to a wheelchair, who four years ago lost her husband. Yet her moments of understandable despair give way to laughter and declarations of love. Battlefield courage is admirable; but sometimes no less praiseworthy is the bravery of those who overcome, every day.

-Rabbi David Wolpe

The Broken Jar

I recently read a book by P.J. Long, a mom who suffered a traumatic brain injury when she fell off a horse. In her book, "Gifts from a Broken Jar", she recounts this story from India about a village boy who brought water to a wealthy man.

"Every day, the boy walked several miles from the village to the river and back again, carrying water in two clay jars, one in his left hand and one in his right. The man paid for the water that was delivered – one full jar and one half full, for the jar in one hand was cracked and its water leaked out along the roadside. Over the long months, the boy made many trips carrying water.

"One day he sat to rest before returning to the river, and a spirit in the cracked jar spoke to him. 'I am sorry, Master, that you have to work harder because of me. If I were perfect like your other jar, you would not need to take so many trips. And you could collect more money too. I am sorry that because of me, your life is made miserable.'

"The boy was surprised to hear such words. He did not think his life was miserable. He replied to the spirit, 'Because of you, I am very lucky. A broken jar makes life beautiful. Come, let me show you.'

"Together they walked back to the river. One side of the path was bare and dusty. But along the other side, where water had trickled down from the broken jar, the way was strewn with wildflowers."

P.J. Long saw the years of her life following her brain injury reflected in this story. Although her recuperation entailed tremendous struggle, she noted the unexpected gifts along the way. She wrote: "Even though things turned out differently than I might have hoped three years ago, truly now I see how a broken jar makes life beautiful."

-Rabbi Ilana Grinblat

Learning To Be Violins

In days of old, a violin maker always chose the wood for his violins from the north side of a forest. That was the side which the wind and the storms had beaten over time. For this reason, whenever he heard the groaning of the trees in the forest at night, he did not feel sorry for them, for they were just learning to be violins.

We too can learn to be violins hewn out of rough wood, while still playing sweet melodies despite the cacophony of life. All it takes is for us to draw our bows on the fiddle, one stroke at a time, starting with a single note.

If we can be like that violin we can persevere. Despite the agony of defeat, ours can be an ode to God, praising God for the victory of joy and love. Joined by our family, by our friends and by this congregation, we can be part of the symphony of life.

-Rabbi Dr. Ed Weinsberg

What Have We Lost, and What Do We Still Have?

I still remember an experience that I had some years ago. I came to a Rabbinical Assembly convention in order to give a major address and when I unpacked in the hotel room, I couldn't find my speech. I rushed out very upset and said to the first person I met, one of my classmates, "I've lost my speech! What am I going to do?" I must have sounded – I know I felt – like the end of the world had come. He put me in my place, quietly but firmly, and enabled me to see my "tsores" in perspective. He quietly said to me, "I just lost my wife." I felt so dumb ... and so ungrateful.

May we be spared from many defeats in this new year. But if face them we must, let us remember our blessings, cherish our family, and may the warmth of those living and the memories of those gone grant us comfort.

-Rabbi Jack Riemer

God's Questions in the Final Exam

Perhaps these questions can help with the only exam that counts in the end.

God Won't Ask ...

1. God won't ask what kind of fancy car you drove. God will ask how many people you took to synagogue who didn't have transportation.

2. God won't ask the square footage of your house. God will ask how many people you helped who didn't have a house.

3. God won't ask how many fancy clothes you had in your closet. God will ask how many of those clothes you gave away to the poor.

4. God won't ask what social class you were in. God will ask what kind of "class" you displayed.

5. God won't ask how many material possessions you had. God will ask whether those material possessions dictated your life.

6. God won't ask you what your highest salary was. God will ask if you trampled over any people to obtain that salary.

7. God won't ask how much overtime you worked. God will ask if you worked overtime for your community.

8. God won't ask how many promotions you received. God will ask what you did to promote others.

9. God won't ask what your job title was. God will ask if you performed your job to the best of your ability.

10. God won't ask how many promotions you took to chase a dollar bill. God will ask how many promotions you refused to advance your family's quality of life.

-Anonymous

If I Had My Life to Live Over

I would have talked less and listened more.

I would have invited friends over to dinner even if the carpet was stained and the sofa faded.

I would have eaten the popcorn in the "good" living room and worried much less about the dirt when someone wanted to light fire in the fireplace.

I would have taken the time to listen to my grandfather ramble about his youth.

I would never have insisted the car windows be rolled up on a summer day because my hair had just been teased and sprayed.

I would have burned the pink candle sculpted like a rose before it melted in storage.

I would have sat on the lawn with my children and not worried about grass stains.

I would have cried and laughed less while watching television and more while watching life.

I would have shared more of the responsibility carried by my husband.

I would have gone to bed when I was sick instead of pretending the earth would go into a holding pattern if I weren't there for the day.

I would never have bought anything just because it was practical, wouldn't show soil, or was guaranteed to last a lifetime.

Instead of wishing away nine months of pregnancy, I'd have cherished every moment and realized that the wonderment growing inside me was the only chance in life to assist God in a miracle.

When my kids kissed me impetuously, I would never have said, "Later. Now go get washed up for dinner."

There would have been more "I love yous"... more "I'm sorrys"... but mostly, given another shot at life, I would seize every minute ... look at it and really see it ... live it ... and never give it back.

Don't forget to stop and smell the roses today! Take time to tell a loved one how much you love them, do something nice for yourself, and stop to give God thanks for all of it.

-Erma Bombeck, "Eat Less Cottage Cheese and More Ice Cream"

Transforming Our Weakness Into Strength

In 1931, the French composer Maurice Ravel wrote two piano concertos. The first was conventional, the second written for one hand. An important pianist had suffered a calamity, the loss of his right hand. In a resolution of genius and affection, Ravel composed the "Piano Concerto for the Left Hand and Orchestra."

It was not an artistic compromise for an emotional impulse. The composition became a standard of style and disciplined beauty. Every time I hear it, there is a response of excitement and awe – the power of a person to rescue beauty from tragedy. To rise above. To transform a weakness into strength. Is there a greater art in the human experience?

-Rabbi Arnold Turetsky

Before I Go

When my life has reached its very end,
And I take that final breath;
I want to know I've left behind,
Some "good" before my death.

I hope that in my final hour,
In all honesty I can say:
That somewhere in my lifetime,
I have brightened someone's day.

That maybe I have brought a smile
To someone else's face,
And made one moment a little sweeter
While they dwelled here in this place.

Lord, please be my reminder
And whisper softly in my ear ...
To be a "giver," not a "taker,"
In the years I have left here.

Give to me the strength I need,
Open up my mind and my soul ...
That I might show sincere compassion,
And love to others before I go.

For if not a heart be touched by me,
And not a smile was left behind ...
Then the life that I am blessed with,
Will have been a waste of time.

With all my heart, I truly hope
To leave something here on earth ...
That touched another, made them smile
And gave to my life ... worth.

-Anonymous

How Do You Live Your Dash?

I read of a man who stood to speak at the funeral of a friend.

He referred to the dates on her tombstone from the beginning ... to the end.

He noted that first came her date of birth and spoke the following date with tears, but he said what mattered most of all was the dash between those years 1934-1998.

For that dash represents all the time that she spent alive on earth ... and now only those who loved her know what that little line is worth.

For it matters not how much we own: the cars ... the house ... the cash, what matters is how we live and love and how we spend our dash.

So think about this long and hard ... are there things you'd like to change? For you never know how much time is left. That can still be rearranged.

If we could just slow down enough to consider what's true and real and always try to understand the way other people feel.

And be less quick to anger, and show appreciation more and love the people in our lives like we've never loved before.

If we treat each other with respect, and more often wear a smile ... remembering that this special dash might only last a little while.

So, when your eulogy's being read with your life's actions to rehash ... would you be proud of the things they say about how you spent your dash?

-Unknown

What I Have Learned

Gabriel Garcia Marquez' "100 Years of Solitude" told a story about life, death, magic and mystery that could not be improved upon. Garcia Marquez, a Colombian, won the Nobel Prize; it was worldly recognition for a literary genius, a true master. He has dropped from public view because Garcia Marquez has a cancer of the lymphatic system that is getting worse.

As a final gift to his friends he sent this farewell letter. Through the ubiquity of the Internet, it has found its way to others. This is a reflection whose wisdom will inspire you to live and relish your life. It would be a sin for me to abbreviate this astounding blessing.

"If for an instant God were to forget that I am a rag doll and gifted me with a piece of life, possibly I wouldn't say all that I think, but rather I would think of all that I say. I would value things, not for their worth but for what they mean. I would sleep little, dream more, understanding that for each minute we close our eyes we lose sixty seconds of light.

I would walk when others hold back, I would wake when others sleep. I would listen when others talk, and how I would enjoy a good chocolate ice cream! If God were to give me a piece of life, I would dress simply, throw myself face first into the sun, baring not only my body but also my soul. My God, if I had a heart, I would write my hate on ice, and wait for the sun to show. Over the stars I would paint with a Van Gogh dream a Benedetti poem, and a Serrat song would be the serenade I'd offer to the moon. With my tears I would water roses, to feel the pain of their thorns, and the red kiss of their petals ...

My God, if I had a piece of life... I wouldn't let a single day pass without telling the people I love that I love them. I would convince each woman and each man that they are my favorites, and I would live in love with love. I would show men how very wrong they are to think that they cease to be in love when they grow old, not knowing that they grow old when they cease to be in love! To a child I shall give wings, but I shall let him learn to fly on his own. I would teach the old that death does not come with old age, but with forgetting. So much have I learned from you, oh men ...

I have learned that everyone wants to live on the peak of the mountain, without knowing that real happiness is in how it is scaled. I have learned that when a newborn child squeezes for the first time with his tiny fist his father's finger, he has him trapped forever. I have learned that a man has the right to look down on another only when he has to help the other get to his feet....

-Gabriel Garcia Marquez

Which Are You?

A daughter complained to her father about her life and how things were so hard for her. She did not know how she was going to make it and wanted to give up. She was tired of fighting and struggling. It seemed as one problem was solved a new one arose.

Her father, a chef, took her to the kitchen. He filled three pots with water and placed each on a high fire. Soon the pots came to a boil.

In one he placed carrots, in the second he placed eggs, and the last he placed ground coffee beans. He let them sit and boil, without saying a word.

The daughter sucked her teeth and impatiently waited, wondering what he was doing. In about twenty minutes he turned off the burners. He fished the carrots out and placed them in a bowl. He pulled the eggs out and placed them a bowl. Then he ladled the coffee out and placed it in a bowl.

Turning to her he asked. "Darling, what do you see?"

"Carrots, eggs, and coffee," she replied.

He brought her closer and asked her to feel the carrots. She did and noted that they were soft. He then asked her to take an egg and break it. After pulling off the shell, she observed the hard-boiled egg. Finally, he asked her to sip the coffee. She smiled as she tasted its rich aroma.

She humbly asked. "What does it mean Father?"

He explained that each of them had faced the same adversity, boiling water, but each reacted differently.

The carrot went in strong, hard, and unrelenting. But after being subjected to the boiling water, it softened and became weak.

The egg had been fragile. Its thin outer shell had protected its liquid interior. But after sitting through the boiling water, its inside became hardened.

The ground coffee beans were unique, however. After they were in the boiling water, they had changed the water.

"Which are you?" he asked his daughter. "When adversity knocks on your door, how do you respond? Are you a carrot, an egg, or a coffee bean?"

Are you the carrot that seems hard, but with pain and adversity do you wilt and become soft and lose your strength?

Are you the egg, which starts off with a malleable heart? Were you a fluid spirit, but after a death, a breakup, a divorce, or a layoff have you become hardened and stiff. Your shell looks the same, but are you bitter and tough with a stiff spirit and heart?

Or are you like the coffee bean? The bean changes the hot water, the thing that is bringing the pain, to its peak flavor reaches 212 degrees Fahrenheit. When the water gets the hottest, it just tastes better.

If you are like the coffee bean, when things are at their worst, you get better and make things better around you.

How do you handle adversity? Are you a carrot, an egg, or coffee?

-Anonymous

A Thought for the New Year: The Holiness of Time

What shall we do with time that is ours now? Professor Abraham Joshua Heschel left us an important clue when he wrote: "Judaism is a religion of time, aiming at the sanctification of time."

Yes, we can sanctify time. Not only is Rosh Hashanah a holy day, and Yom Kippur and Shabbat, but every day is holy if we choose to sanctify it. Remember the weekday to keep it holy.

How does time become holy? It becomes holy when a part of it is given to others, when we share and care and listen. Time is sanctified when we use it–to forgive and ask forgiveness; to remember things too long forgotten and to forget things too long remembered; to reclaim sacred things too casually abandoned and to abandon shabby things too highly cherished; to remember that life's most crucial question is–how are we using time?

Yes, time flies but we are the navigators. More important than counting time is making time count.

As we face the new year there is a special urgency to the prayer of the Psalmist: "Teach us to number our days so that we may attain a heart of wisdom."

-Rabbi Sidney Greenberg

Yizkor

It just might be the most well known and observed of synagogue services – it is Yizkor. We tend, erroneously, to focus on the past aspect of memory, but truth be told, the word *yizkor* is written in the future tense.

In a brilliant essay, former chief rabbi of England, Lord Immanuel Jacobovits observed that the word, Yizkor, is recorded in the Hebrew Bible six times – all of them bespeak a message – not to the one who passed away, but rather, to the ones who live on. In a word, yizkor is not relegated to the past, it carries a pregnant meaning for the future.

When the famed Yiddish writer, Sholom Aleichem passed away, he left instructions in his will that his family was to gather on his yahrzeit to read one of his funny stories. They were not allowed to be mournful or morose – they were to laugh. In fact, he said, that if they were incapable of laughing they should not gather.

In a biography of one of the rabbinic giants of the 20th century, Rabbi Moshe Feinstein, we find a strange vignette. It seems that once Reb Moshe, as he was affectionately called, made a shiva call to three brothers who were mourning the passing of their beloved father. At a certain point, this preeminent scholar and sage asked what they had each inherited. A rather unusual and out of line question from anyone – let alone from one who was considered to be the rabbi of the generation par excellence.

Noticing the perplexity and confusion on their faces, Reb Moshe explained more or less as follows: "Your father, single handedly, supported a home for orphans. He also was a major funder of a soup kitchen and he was a lead philanthropist of a certain yeshiva. I am simply asking, which one of the three are each of you going to inherit as your special mitzva."

Yes, the loss of a loved one is devastating and leaves a gaping whole that can't fully be filled – but there usually is a path that was charted by the deceased that can be followed – sometimes in the communal arena, sometimes in the personal.

Is one allowed to feel wistful and tearful when recalling loved ones? Of course – in fact, one's humanity and sensitivity might be called into question if not. But at the same time, one should feel a sense of deep love and profound hope at the chance to be, please G-d, a link in the indissoluble chain of our people and as an inheritor of these special people we call, family.

-Rabbi David Gutterman

Making the Most of Life

On July 26, 1986, at Tanglewood, the 14-year-old Japanese violinist Midori played Leonard Bernstein's Serenade for Violin and String Orchestra. Bernstein conducted the orchestra at that concert. The performance was described by John Rockwell of The New York Times as being "technically near-perfect." During the fifth movement, a string broke on Midori's violin. She continued on the violin given her by the concertmaster. Suddenly a string broke on that violin as well. She then continued on the violin that the associate concertmaster gave her. John Rockwell wrote, "When it was over, audience, orchestra and conductor-composer joined in giving her a cheering, stomping, whistling ovation." Two days later, during an interview, Midori said, "What could I do? My strings broke, and I didn't want to stop the music.'"

Whether it is Midori, or any other soloist, the ability to restore the musical moment to perfection following the breaking of a string is a model of how to live our lives. When things are going well for us, we feel wonderful. But what happens when the unexpected intrudes upon the moment? What is our reaction? Do we throw up our hands in defeat? Can we restore the music of our lives? Do we use the interrupted moment to intensify the beauty that was there before as we go forward? Can we again become one with the music? How does this play out over the course of our lives?

William Butler Yeats composed a poem ("Among School Children") about the process of living and aging, about the contrast between youth and age, The critic Helen Vendler wrote, "The poem is written the day after Yeats's sixty-first birthday, as Yeats, looking retrospectively at his life, asks: If all life ends in disappointment, deformity, disillusion, and death, is there anything at all to be said for having lived?" The answer, Vendler points out, is in the final stanza:

VIII

> Labour is blossoming or dancing where
> The body is not bruised to pleasure soul,
> Nor beauty born out of its own despair,
> Nor blear-eyed wisdom out of midnight oil.
> O chestnut-tree, great-rooted blossomer,
> Are you the leaf, the blossom or the bole?
> O body swayed to music, O brightening glance,
> How can we know the dancer from the dance?

Vendler explains that while we do not compose the music, we choreograph our own dance in response to the music, a dance that "is continually refreshed over a lifetime as the ever-brightening glance conceives successive steps in response to the music." Yeats sees no difference between the self and the choreography "it invents and adapts to the music of time," Vendler teaches that Yeats "redefines the attitude to be taken toward life. One is the dance one traces; and each year of living is indispensable to the ultimate line of the choreography." In writing "O body swayed to music," Yeats is not saying "that one has forgotten the disappointments of love, devotion, affection, and wisdom-seeking, but that they have been assimilated into the ceaseless creative dance of personally-invented selfhood."

When we look at our lives, can we see only the brokenness and disappointments? Or do we adjust our steps and continue to sway with the music. The choice of reaction to the broken strings of our lives is ours.

-Rabbi Stephan O. Parnes

Know Your Strength

From your challenges you may know your strengths.

You did not make yourself. You did not choose your parents, nor did you design the environment that nurtured you.

The One who brought you to this world, who knew you before you were conceived and who fashioned you in the womb – He knew intimately all the challenges you would meet, your faults, your struggles. He was the one who designed they should be there.

And for each brick wall, He provided you a ladder. For each chasm a bridge. For each mountain a deep reserve of superhuman strength to surprise even your own self.

When one of those challenges arises, you need only imagine what it must take to overcome – and you can be confident that strength is within you.

-Rabbi Menachem Mendel Schneerson

No Petitioner Ever Succeeded in Ransoming Anything From the Captivity of Yesterday

This will be the first High Holidays without my father. We'll feel his absence acutely in our family, especially at the blowing of the shofar on Rosh Hashanah because he was an outstanding

Ba'al Tekiah, and on Yom Kippur at the Shema Kolenu prayer which he loved and which, in recent years, particularly moved him. At the same time, though, I'm sure that we'll feel especially close to him. I remember asking for his blessing just before Kol Nidrei last year, then walking to Shul with a great sense of sadness, perhaps unconsciously knowing that this would be the final time I would receive it from his hands.

I imagine that we all feel similarly at this season about the dead whom we have loved. We experience both their physical absence – they aren't here at the table, we go to Shul without them – and their spiritual presence as part of some greater whole: they're there, they belong in that great expanse of time which encompasses the many generations for whom these days have been holy.

This points to an important paradox at the heart of the High Holydays. Our hour is brief; the years flee ever more quickly away, what's past is gone inexorably. No petitioner ever succeeded in ransoming anything from the captivity of yesterday. Yet our life also belongs to a far greater whole across a much broader expanse of time. We stand at the intersection between the dead and the unborn whose lives stretch out behind us and before us. We participate in a vast chain of existence; our own life is only a fragment in the huge continuum which includes all living beings and which is in turn enfolded in the unending vitality of God.

Avitah Tehilah is a beautiful prayer which expresses this duality, – how short our days are, yet how vast is the greater life to which they belong: "You, God, desire praise from flesh and blood, from a passing shadow ... from human beings who die in judgment and live by your mercy and ascribe glory to you, life of all the worlds." Our life withers like grass, yet our existence is deeply significant, because "Your glory, God, rests upon us." Briefly, we partake of eternity.

Such a double vision helps us to focus on what really matters on this earth. When we remember how fragile our life is, we realize that we have to use it intensely. There's no time to waste; we must get on with dedicating our energy, focusing our values, giving our love, healing the wounds between us. When we think of the great chain of existence of which we are part, we feel nourished and inspired in our tasks. For the deepest desire of our spirit is to be pure, generous, worthy of the privilege of belonging, if even for a moment, to this vast expanse of sacred life.

The infinite instructs the time-bound: we know how we must live.

-Rabbi Jonathan Wittenberg

We're Stronger Than We Think

A little boy went to the fair with his dad and saw an inflatable clown sporting a sign that read, "Try to knock me down." He hit it, he slapped it, he pushed it – he struck it again and again, and the harder he hit, the quicker it seemed to bounce back up. No matter how hard he tried, it just would not stay down. His father watched as the boy punched the clown until he finally interrupted and asked, "How is it possible for the clown to keep standing back up, no matter how hard you hit it?"

The child scratched his head and said, "Dad, I think this clown is standing up on the inside."

Did you know that each of us has the ability to stand up on the inside? Let me explain. A magazine article told about a woman in rural Florida who was recuperating from a lengthy illness. She enjoyed sitting on her front porch in her wheelchair and, on this day, she watched her son repair his automobile. He raised it on blocks of wood, removed the tires and slid on his back underneath the vehicle.

Suddenly there was a loud crack and the automobile lurched to one side, pinning the young man underneath. She screamed for her husband who ran to assist, but he couldn't budge the car or the young man. He climbed into his own vehicle and sped off for help.

The mother, who hadn't walked in months, realized that her son's groans were growing fainter and she knew that it would be up to her to save the boy. She sensed he was dying and that she had to act immediately.

She rose to her feet and walked on shaky legs to the car. Bracing herself, she lifted. The car rose a few inches – just enough to let the boy scramble free. Then she collapsed.

After a thorough examination, she was found only to have suffered strained muscles. And the incredulous doctor's words were most telling: "I will always wonder," he said, "how far she might have lifted that car if she had been well and strong."

We've read similar stories about persons exhibiting almost super-human strength in times of crises. Call it a miracle. Call it providence. Or call it a physiological response to an adrenalin surge – this mother, and others like her, found the strength she needed, when she needed it, to face the crisis at hand.

And so it is with all of us. When life knocks us down and it seems impossible to get back up, when life demands more from us than we are able to give, then more than ever, we need to find a way to do what needs to be done. It is at just these times that we come face to face with a reserve of strength we never knew we had.

We are stronger than we think. Like the clown, we, too, have the ability to bounce back. We have emotional, spiritual and even physical resources at our disposal. We may get knocked down, but we don't have to stay down.

It's like standing up on the inside. And when we find strength to do that, we will be able to stand up to most anything life throws our way.

-Steve Goodier

A Decision I Must Make Every Day

Gretchen Alexander is sightless. But she refuses to allow her blindness to limit her life activities. She enjoys archery, golf, softball, sailing and water-skiing, as well as a number of other activities that those of us who are sighted have yet to learn.

She also speaks to groups about living life fully. When speaking to a group of high school students, she was once asked if there was anything she wouldn't try.

"I've decided to never skydive," she answered. "It would scare the heck out of my dog."

Why do some people rise above their problems and live life fully, while others become defeated? Merle Shain explains it this way: "There are only two ways to approach life, as a victim or as a gallant fighter. And every day the decision is ours." Or put another way, we can believe we're helpless or we can believe we're powerful and capable. And every day we reaffirm our belief.

Another person who knew what it was like to live sightless, not to mention soundless, was Helen Keller. She famously pointed out that "although the world is full of suffering, it is also full of the overcoming of suffering." Does that sound someone who believes she is helpless, or like someone who believes she is capable?

I love the perspective of a shop owner in Nottingham, England. He posted this notice in the window of his coat store: "We have been established for over 100 years and have been pleasing and displeasing customers ever since. We have made money and lost money, suffered the effects of coal nationalization, coat rationing, government control and bad payers. We have been cussed and discussed, messed about, lied to, held up, robbed and swindled. The only reason we stay in business is to see what happens next." Though he lifts up a myriad of hardships they've endured, they somehow figured out how to stay in business. Does that sound like someone who believes he is helpless ... or capable?

When discouraged, some people will give up, give in or give out far too early. They blame their problems on difficult situations, unreasonable people or their own inabilities.

When discouraged, other people will push back that first impulse to quit, push down their initial fear, push through feelings of helplessness and push ahead. They're less likely to find something to blame and more likely to find a way through.

For me, it's an important decision about whether I want to live my life fully and with courage or whether I will be forever defeated by harsh circumstances. It's a decision about believing I am powerful enough and capable enough. And it's a decision I must make every day of my life.

-Steve Goodier

Overcoming

Remember the story of the king who had the perfect diamond? He dropped it and a crack developed the length of the stone. The King promised great riches to the man who repaired it. A wise old jeweler knew that a crack cannot be erased, so he carved petals on top of the diamond. Now the crack formed the stem of a blossom. The crack did not disappear but it was transformed. We will never be perfect; but with repentance and resolve we can turn flaws into flowers.

-Rabbi David Wolpe

I Wish You Enough

Recently, I overheard a mother and daughter in their last moments together at the airport as the daughter's departure had been announced. Standing near the security gate, they hugged and the mother said: "I wish you enough."

The daughter replied, "Mom, our life together has been more than enough. Your love is all I ever needed. I wish you enough, too, Mom." They kissed and the daughter left.

The mother walked over to the window where I sat. Standing there, I could see she wanted and needed to cry.

I tried not to intrude on her privacy but she welcomed me in by asking, "Did you ever say good-bye to someone knowing it would be forever?" "Yes, I have," I replied. "Forgive me for asking but why is this a forever good-bye?"

"I am old and she lives so far away. I have challenges ahead and the reality is the next trip back will be for my funeral," she said.

When you were saying good-bye, I heard you say, "I wish you enough." May I ask what that means?"

She began to smile. "That's a wish that has been handed down from other generations. My parents used to say it to everyone." She paused a moment and looked up as if trying to remember it in detail and she smiled even more.

"When we said 'I wish you enough' we were wanting the other person to have a life filled with just enough good things to sustain them". Then turning toward me, she shared the following, reciting it from memory,

I wish you enough sun to keep your attitude bright.
I wish you enough rain to appreciate the sun more.

I wish you enough happiness to keep your spirit alive.
I wish you enough pain so that the smallest joys in life
    appear much bigger.
I wish you enough gain to satisfy your wanting.
I wish you enough loss to appreciate all that you possess.
I wish you enough hellos to get you through the
    final good-bye.

She then began to cry and walked away.

They say it takes a minute to find a special person. An hour to appreciate them. A day to love them. And an entire life to forget them.

-Bob Perks

On Loss: Ten Lessons from Sheryl Sandberg's Facebook Post

Dave Goldberg, the husband of Facebook Chief Operating Officer Sheryl Sandberg, died suddenly and unexpectedly in an apparent accident during a family vacation in May 2015. Following the 30-day *sheloshim* period of mourning, Sandberg wrote a Facebook post describing her grief and her response to this tragedy. It is excerpted in the following essay.

"I want to choose life and meaning."

Facebook Chief Operating Officer, Sheryl Sandberg marked the 30th day (*sheloshim*) of her husband's passing in a moving and gut-wrenching post on her Facebook page. I have read it over and over again, and cried, as should you. She is a poignant teacher who turns her loss into powerful lifetime lessons for us.

1. Faith matters. Sandberg honors her religion and waits the prescribed *sheloshim*: "Judaism calls for a period of intense mourning ... after a loved one is buried." She draws on the teaching of a childhood friend, now a rabbi, to relay "the most powerful one-line prayer: 'Let me not die while I am still alive.'"

2. Choices matter. "I think when tragedy occurs, it presents a choice. You can give in to the void, the emptiness that fills

your heart..." But in the tradition of Anne Frank "when I can, I want to choose life and meaning."

3. Making loss matter. In line with the teachings of Viktor Frankl "this is why I am writing: I am sharing what I have learned in the hope that it helps someone else. In the hope that there can be some meaning from this tragedy."

4. Family matters. Even as a COO of a major company, we are replaceable, but not so as a father or a mother: "I have gained a more profound understanding of what it is to be a mother, both through the depth of the agony I feel when my children scream and cry and from the connection my mother has to my pain..."

5. What to say to someone in mourning. Be there. Show up. Your very presence comforts. Avoid avoidance. "Even a simple 'How are you?'– almost always asked with the best of intentions – is better replaced with 'How are you today?' When I am asked 'How are you?' I stop myself from shouting, 'My husband died a month ago, how do you think I am?' When I hear 'How are you today?' I realize the person knows that the best I can do right now is to get through each day."

6. What NOT to say to someone in mourning. "A friend of mine with late-stage cancer told me that the worst thing people could say to him was 'It is going to be okay.' That voice in his head would scream, 'How do you know it is going to be okay? Do you not understand that I might die?' ... When people say to me, 'You and your children will find happiness again,' my heart tells me, Yes, I believe that, but I know I will never feel pure joy again."

7. Community matters. "I have heard from too many women who lost a spouse ... Some lack support networks and struggle alone as they face emotional distress and financial insecurity. It seems so wrong to me that we abandon these women and their families when they are in greatest need."

8. Contributing matters. Find what gives you sense of self. For some it is volunteer work and for others gardening. "For me, starting the transition back to work has been a savior, a chance to feel useful and connected."

9. Gratitude matters. "As heartbroken as I am, I look at my

children each day and rejoice that they are alive. I appreciate every smile, every hug. I no longer take each day for granted."

10. Legacy matters. "Dave, to honor your memory and raise your children as they deserve to be raised, I promise to do all I can..."

Dave Goldberg's life will be celebrated for generations through the expressions of his loving wife, children and the lessons shared through the very social media that Sheryl Sandberg has helped build. May your light continue to shine forever.

-Dr. Afshine Emrani

Chapter Nine

IN OUR HEARTS FOREVER: THE POWER OF REMEMBERING

As time passes after the loss of a loved one, we find that we have an awesome and even fearful power – we can create our loved ones anew through remembering. What do we remember of them; what do we choose to remember, to present to the world around us, to children, grandchildren, even total strangers. If we have money, we might even erect an edifice to their memory, like the Pharaohs of ancient Egypt, perhaps a building at a university, or a library, or a cancer center or theater. More modestly, perhaps we endow a chair at an educational institution, or a scholarship.

Most of us, though, can't engage in such acts of public monument building. We find, however, that our very acts of remembering, of storytelling, and especially recounting and repeating acts of kindness, like serving at the homeless shelter or volunteering at the library or hospital while thinking "This is where my loved one found so much meaning," and perhaps telling a client or two about him or her – all of these perpetuate our loved ones in the world, and cause them to live again for others.

> We thank You, O God of life and love,
> For the resurrecting gift of memory
> Which endows Your children,
> Fashioned in Your image,
> With the Godlike sovereign power
> To give immortality through love.
> Blessed are You, God,
> Who enables Your children to remember.
>
> *-Rabbi Morris Adler*

Gratefulness: A Source of Strength

Nothing can console us when we lose a beloved person and no one should try. We have to simply bear and survive it. That sounds hard but is in fact a great consolation: When the hole remains unfilled, we remain connected through it. It is wrong to say that God fills the gap, because he keeps it empty, and so helps us to sustain our old communion, even through pain.

The more beautiful and fulfilling our memories, the harder the separation. But gratefulness transforms the agony of memory into a quiet joy. We should avoid burrowing in our memories, just as we do not look at a precious gift continuously. Rather, we should rather save them for special hours, like a hidden treasure of which we are certain. Then a pervading joy and strength will flow from the past.

-Dietrich Bonhoeffer

Starlight

There are stars whose light only reaches the earth long after they have fallen apart. There are people whose remembrance gives light in this world, long after they have passed away. This light shines in our darkest nights on the road we must follow.

-Hannah Senesch

Planting and Plucking

Die when we may, I want it said of me, by those who knew me best, that I always plucked a thistle and planted a flower, when I thought a flower would grow.

-Abraham Lincoln

Our Parents and Grandparents – They Are Still With Us

The story is told of a recent Boston marathon in which an old Jewish gentleman in his eighties, born in a small town in Poland, whose doctors advised him not to run, came in with a very respectable record. Spectators standing nearby were astounded. "How did you do it?" they asked.

"How?" he answered, with calm and assurance, and a deep inner faith. "I had companions running with me."

"Who were your companions? We did not see them!"

"You did not see them," he replied, "because they were in my heart, and in my memory. My zadie, *olov hasholom,* ran with me. My father, *olov hasholom,* ran with me. Everyone from the *shtetl* ran with me. *Mir hoben gelayfen tzusammen.* We all ran together!"

Throughout all the highs and lows of life our zadies and bubbies, and our mothers and fathers, and all our dear ones, whether they are sitting or standing next to us, or whether they exist today merely in our heart and in our memory, are running alongside us in everything we do. If we look and notice them, we will always know that their love and support never ends, not even with the grave. They are still running alongside us!

-Adapted from Rabbi Gerald I. Wolpe

Still Warm From an Old Jacket

The late master of Jewish story-telling, Reb Shlomo Carlebach, tells the following tale:

It seems that many years ago a little seven-year-old boy and his family were about to leave their native Poland. The day before their departure the father took the little boy to the town where the Rebbe lived so he could receive the Rebbe's blessing. They remained overnight in the home of the Rebbe, and the little boy slept in the Rebbe' study.

Staring at all the holy books, the little boy could not sleep. In the middle of the night he saw the Rebbe enter the room, and he pretended that he was asleep. The Rebbe whispered "Such a sweet child!" Thinking the child might be cold, the Rebbe took off his coat and placed it lovingly on the sleeping child.

Many years later, when the little boy became an old man of eighty years, when asked what the source of his kindness and comfort was, he said that 73 years ago the Rebbe showed him love and comfort, and placed his coat on him to keep him warm. "I am still warm from that coat," said the eighty-year-old man.

The Yizkor prayers which we recite remind us that at some many occasions in our lives, many people put their warm coats on us, touched us, loved us, comforted us. Their coats still provide warmth for us today – whether they are living or not – and will continue to do so.

From these coats we are still warm, and we thank them for their love and warmth. May their memory be for a blessing.

-D.P.E.

We Live in Deeds

We live in deeds, not years; in thoughts, not breaths;
In feelings, not in figures on a dial.
We should count time by heart-throbs. He most lives
Who thinks most, feels the noblest, acts the best.
And he whose heart beats quickest lives the longest:
Lives in one hour more than in years do some

-James Philip Bailey

From Beyond the Grave
Our Loved Ones Reach Out and Touch Us

Rabbi Eli Schochet, of California, tells a story of his childhood. He grew up in Chicago, where his father and his grandfather were both rabbis. One Sabbath afternoon when he was a young boy at his grandfather's home, a big Cadillac pulled up. Three burly guards stepped out with a well-known Jewish gangster. The man walked in and laid an envelope on the rabbi's table filled with cash. "This is for my mother's yahrzeit." Then he left. (On the yahrzeit in memory of a beloved parent or others, it is a special Jewish religious obligation to give charity.)

Eli was angry at his grandfather. "We do not touch money on the Sabbath. How can you accept money from that man, on the Sabbath of all times?"

His grandfather softly answered, "Don't you understand what happened? This man is a criminal who lives an ugly life. But for one brief moment he looked on a calendar and saw that it was his mother's yahrzeit. He remembered his mother's dreams for him, that he grow up to be a Jew, that he grow up to be a *mentsch*. For one brief moment, he wants her memory to live within. That was a sacred moment, and I do not want to take away from it."

That story says it all. Even from beyond the grave, our loved ones can reach out and touch us, and change us.

-Rabbi Michael Gold

A Yizkor Guided Imagery Exercise

Yizkor is brief. Following a few prayers, we are left with moments of silence to think about those who were closest to us. What should we do during those moments? How should we best remember those who no longer walk this earth?

During these silent moments let's take a journey into the hearts of our loved ones. Close your eyes, and imagine walking into a room, perhaps a room in the home in which you grew up. Now shut the door and envision your beloved father or mother, husband or wife, sister or brother, son or daughter, other relative or friend. Look into their eyes, touch their hands and feel their skin. Listen to their voices.

Let's speak with our loved ones. What do we want to say that we didn't when they were alive?

Perhaps we will say "I am a new mother" or "new father" and then introduce them to the child they never met. Or, show them how their little grandchild has grown since they left. We may share professional news. Maybe we will say "thank you for all you did." We might apologize for hurting them or grant *them* forgiveness. Or we might simply say "I love you and miss you so very, very deeply."

During these moments see them, hear them, touch them. And make peace with yourself, your beloved and with God. Then you will have transformed these ordinary moments into sacred moments.

A man who lost his mother this year told me that he would give anything just to have a few more minutes with her. Yizkor provides those minutes.

-Rabbi David Woznica, from Rabbi Elie Spitz

We Have Our Ancestors at Our Side

Steven Spielberg presented us with a gift of American historical memory. He told us the story of the uprising on the slave ship Amistad. In the pivotal scene John Quincy Adams, a former President, finally agrees to represent Cinque and the other slaves who by chance had been imprisoned in New England, and needed a lawyer to defend their freedom.

In the film, unshackled at Adams's command, Cinqué strolls with the former President through his greenhouse – admiring, pointedly, an African violet – and then confers with the "chief," assuring him through a translator: We have my ancestors at our side. I will call into the past, far back to the beginning of time, and beg them to come help me at the judgment. I will reach back and draw them into me.

Hear, again, the words Cinque spoke: "We have ... ancestors at our side ... I will reach back and draw them into me." As Jews we can also say on Yom Kippur: "we have ancestors at our side." And what is the function of Yizkor, of memory: "I will reach back and draw them into me."

This is the meaning of Yom Kippur: Taking the gifts granted us by those who have touched our lives, and drawing those gifts into our life. And to do this as individuals, each of us with personal memories. And to do this as a people, with our collective memory.

-Unknown

Names Written in Our Hearts

For many, the most moving moments of Yom Kippur come when we pause to offer the Yizkor prayers. It's a moment of defining who we are by proclaiming the names of the people who made us who we are. And as we do so, we remember the things they taught us. We feel their presence and we know that we are not here alone. If we ever stopped proclaiming those names, not only would they be lost to oblivion, we'd also be lost. Then we would really be alone. If we couldn't count on future generations of Jews promising to offer our names when the time comes, we'd feel that we had no future, no promise of immortality.

[Rabbi Matthew Simon writes that:] My favorite theologian, Ira Berkow, the sports editor of the New York Times, told me more than I wanted to know about the owner of the Chicago Bulls, Jerry Reinsdorf. Ira Berkow wrote earlier this year, "On the desk in the office of Jerry Reinsdorf, Reinsdorf is quick to remind, is this framed axiom, 'Nothing is written in stone.'"

At Yizkor we know that is false. Some day Jerry Reinsdorf's name will be written in stone. Names of our beloved are written in stone on their graves. Their names are written in bronze on yahrzeit plaques, and on annual announcements of their date of death. Their names are written in our hearts, and today we reach back and draw them into our memory. But we have been given their gifts. And we have their gifts to give to our children and grandchildren.

-Rabbi Matthew Simon

Father

I used to be a part of you
    belong to you
    the extension of your being
    but now
    you live within me
    are the spark of my consciousness

I say Kaddish for you
    with you
    as you
    sing your melodies
    speak your words
    hearing your voice in mine
    and my eyes
    too green
    have somehow started to reflect
    the blue of yours

I used to be a part of you
    protected by your presence

by your light
but now
the time is mine
and alone

I must be more than myself
    your son
    has become your heir
    has become you

-Menachem Z. Rosensaft

How Am I Going To Comfort Myself?

Rabbi Shlomo Carlebach, may he rest in peace, tells the story of a secular Israeli Professor of Literature, who was quite infamous in Israel among the religious, for loudly proclaiming that religion was foolish, that Jerusalem was not any holier than Tokyo, and that only fools cared about Jewish ritual and tradition. Some secular Israelis are really secular.

Anyway, the story goes that one day he shows up in a Hasidic rebbe's office and says that he wanted to devote his life to religious education. The rabbi asked him whether he was pulling his leg or being sincere, and the professor said, "I'm being very sincere and let me tell you the story."

"During the Yom Kippur War, I was up on the Golan and I was wounded. As I lay bleeding, I realized I was going to die in a couple of hours if I wasn't found. So I began thinking, how am I going to comfort myself for these last two hours of my life? I'm a professor of English Literature, so think about Shakespeare. I tried, and that didn't do it. Then I tried to think of all the philosophy about death and dying that I knew, and that didn't do it. What I couldn't keep out of my memory was my zadie in his big tallis draped down his back, holding my hand and walking to shul on Yom Kippur.

"Then, next came my fondest memory as a little boy, was being on my father's shoulders, dancing at Simhat Torah. Then I remembered I would smell the smells of the seder table, of the chicken soup and gefilte fish with my bubbie and my mother. And all those gave me so much comfort. I began to feel like, my children and grandchildren, what would comfort them in their last two hours of life? They won't have these memories because I didn't give them to them. Then I began thinking, 'Is it only the last two hours of life that one should live with these holy memories? Shouldn't one have them throughout one's life?'

"So, I vowed there to God that if I should be saved, I would devote my life to Jewish education and live Jewishly. Next thing I knew, I woke up in the hospital, having been saved by comrades who found me, and that's why I'm here."

-D.P.E.

The Family Reunion

The family reunion is an event that punctuates and dramatizes the flow of our lives.

Children are born, they grow up,
Our own parents pass on, friends die.
It is growing late, it is years since we began,
And we hardly remember growing older!

At the family reunion we look from the oldest member,
Who may not be present next time,
To the youngest, who was not here last time.
We suddenly glimpse our lives
As a trajectory in time
Beginning at one point and ending at another.

To a higher network of interconnecting arcs.
Life is not only a series of experiences;
It is a whole-real, objective, and unique.
Life is a process of tracing on sand.
With some patterns deeper; larger and more beautiful.

Yet the wind and water ultimately wash over all.
By the same process, time constantly erases its own surface
While forming a deeper structure we never see.

For beneath the sand there is rock

Constantly being shaped by our lives-by our tracings in sand.
At the family reunion the great chain of generations
Threads its way to the present moment,
Linking the old to the young, the dead to the unborn.
It contains – and is contained – by our own life.

As human beings, we are born into a family.
We live without and within it; we color it and shape it,
We bring to the family our gifts, our acts, our children,
Shaping it with all the days of our lives –
And even with our inevitable passage into eternal life.

-Rabbi Arnold M. Goodman

Memory: To Touch a Name

I never fail to walk the memorial plaques of synagogues that I visit. They are like tombstones. They are the historical treasure of the Jews who have passed on, and who found a home and rest and peace within the synagogue. Their names mark the wall, although they are long gone.

In my own congregation, I am proud of the plaques that begin with the 1800s. As we enter the twenty-first century the children of my congregation will be able to touch a name and date that goes back, for them, before time itself.

Each name is a story, a life, a memory that we have been asked to treasure and remember for the year of their death and for the yahrzeits that follow.

-Rabbi Matthew Simon

Memory – Your Greatest Treasure

Many people complain that their memory is not what it used to be. But memory can be a powerful tool for spiritual and emotional rejuvenation!

I once attended a conference at a retreat center in the Rocky Mountains. We were given a long break one afternoon to relax and rejuvenate our spirits. Many of the attendees decided to play golf and asked if I wanted to come along.

Golf does not rejuvenate my spirit. I've LOST more religion on the golf course than I can remember! I feel a bit like Bob Hope who said that if you watch a sport, it's fun; if you play a sport, it's recreation; and if you work at a sport, it's golf." I decided to do something more relaxing, so I went for a walk.

A little way down a secluded, dirt road, I spotted horses in a corral. I carefully approached, so as not to frighten them. Then I inhaled as deeply as I could. With the smell of the horses and the corral came a flood of memories.

I visited my grandparents' guest ranch every summer as a child. When I was a teenager, I worked on the ranch. Some of my happiest memories growing up were around horses and horse smells.

Inhaling horse smells, I recalled hot afternoons of pulling saddles and blankets off perspiring horses then brushing down their backs. The pungent smell of horse sweat filled my mind.

I recalled the soft touch of a horse's nose sniffing my hand for sugar, and the warmth of a horse's neck as I put my arms around it and hugged it close.

Manure smells brought back memories of hours spent in corrals saddling, bridling and working with horses. Again, I inhaled deeply.

I recalled rising before dawn and riding in the crisp, early morning air searching along hills and valleys for horses let out the previous evening to range free of fences.

I remembered afternoon naps under a Ponderosa pine tree, my hat pulled down over my face, listening to the sounds of buzzing flies and swishing horse tails.

As I breathed in the smells, my mind enjoyed ancient memories of day long horseback rides, valley vistas of soft, green grass, brown later in the summer, pristine mountains and clear, shallow mountain creeks running beside horse trails carved in red earth.

I remembered, too, how it felt to be young with my whole life ahead. I felt again the sense of adventure and excitement of those heady, teen years. Not that I'd ever want to go back and relive them – but maybe visit occasionally in my mind. I remembered ... and felt renewed.

Later in the day we shared how we spent our afternoon.

Many people in our group boasted of golf scores. Some talked about walking or hiking. When it was my turn, I said that I had an extraordinary time. "I smelled the horses."

What do you find yourself remembering? Do you often recall times that you would rather forget? Or do you dwell on those memories that bring you joy and inner peace? When you think of the past, is it with regret or with pleasure? What do you remember most: painful times or happy occasions?

Your thoughts can sap your emotions or they can flood your mind with strength-giving energy. Your good memories can rejuvenate your spirit with new life. They can be a solace during difficult times and a source of joy anytime you choose to visit.

Some memories are best forgotten; others may need time to heal. But good memories are like a treasure nobody can steal.

Keep them close. Visit them often. Enjoy.

-*Steve Goodier*

A Mother's Crown

Heaven lit up with a mighty presence,
as the Angels all looked down.
Today the Lord was placing the jewels
Into my mother's crown.

He held up a golden crown,
as my darling mother looked on.
He said in His gentle voice,
'I will now explain each one.'

'The first gem,' He said, 'is a Ruby,
and it's for endurance alone,
for all the nights you waited up
for your children to come home.'
'For all the nights by their bedside,
you stayed till the fever went down.
For nursing every little wound,
I add this ruby to your crown.'

'An emerald, I'll place by the ruby,
for leading your child in the right way.
For teaching them the lessons,
That made them who they are today.'
'For always being right there,
through all life's important events.
I give you a sapphire stone,
for the time and love you spent.'

'For untying the strings that held them,
when they grew up and left home.
I give you this one for courage.'
Then the Lord added a garnet stone.

'I'll place a stone of amethyst,' He said.
'For all the times you spent on your knees,
when you asked if I'd take care of your children,
and then for having faith in Me.'

'I have a pearl for every little sacrifice
that you made without them knowing.
For all the times you went without,
to keep them happy, healthy and growing.'

'And last of all I have a diamond,
the greatest one of all,
for sharing unconditional love
whether they were big or small.'
'It was your love, that helped them grow
Feeling safe and happy and proud
A love so strong and pure
It could shift the darkest cloud.'

After the Lord placed the last jewel in,
He said, 'Your crown is now complete,
You've earned your place in Heaven
With your children at your feet.'

-Rabbi Bernhard Rosenberg

Only a Dad

Only a dad with a tired face,
Coming home from the daily race,
Bringing little of gold or fame
To show how well he has played the game;
But glad in his heart that his own rejoice
To see him come and to hear his voice.

Only a dad with a brood of four,
One of ten million men or more
Plodding along in the daily strife,
Bearing the whips and the scorns of life,
With never a whimper of pain or hate,
For the sake of those who at home await.

Only a dad, neither rich nor proud,
Merely one of the surging crowd,
Toiling, striving from day to day,
Facing whatever may come his way,
Silent whenever the harsh condemn,
And bearing it all for the love of them.

Only a dad but he gives his all,
To smooth the way for his children small,
Doing with courage stern and grim
The deeds that his father did for him.
This is the line that for him I pen:
Only a dad, but the best of men.

-Edgar A. Guest (1916)

Before I Was Myself

Before I was myself you made me, me
With love and patience, discipline and tears,
Then bit by bit stepped back to set me free,
Allowing me to sail upon my sea,
Though well within the headlands of your fears.
Before I was myself you made me, me

With dreams enough of what I was to be
And hopes that would be sculpted by the years,
Then bit by bit stepped back to set me free,
Relinquishing your powers gradually
To let me shape myself among my peers.
Before I was myself you made me, me,
For love inspires learning naturally:
The mind assents to what the heart reveres.
And so it was through love you made me, me
By slowly stepping back to set me free.

-Anonymous

When All That's Left Is Love

When I die
If you need to weep
Cry for someone
Walking the street beside you.
You can love me most by letting
Hands touch hands, and Souls touch souls.
You can love me most by
Sharing your *simchas* and
Multiplying your *mitzvot*.
You can love me most by
Letting me live in your eyes
And not on your mind.
And when you say Kaddish for me
Remember what our
Torah teaches,
Love doesn't die People do.
So when all that's left of me is love
Give me away.

-Rabbi Allen S. Maller

Chapter Ten

A LIGHT TO THE LIVING:
BRINGING A LOVED ONE'S GIFTS TO THE WORLD

Avital part of memory is action. What actions do our memories of loved ones inspire? And what actions do we want our own lives to inspire? Judaism (and other religious traditions as well) stress drawing out the lessons we have learned from our lives or from the lives of others. Jews have a long tradition of writing ethical wills (an example of which appears below), the product of our *heshbon nefesh,* or inner reckoning, to point these lessons out to our surviving families. Another tradition is giving *tzedakah* or doing acts of lovingkindness, inspired by the example of our loved one, or to set an example for our own families.

Passing the Torch

"Aaron did so; he set up the lamps so that they faced forward on the lampstand, just as the LORD commanded Moses."

-Numbers 8:3

I was recently at a funeral on the Mount of Olives in Jerusalem for a Jewish man from New York. He had lived a long life and died peacefully. Yet when his son read his eulogy, everyone had tears in their eyes. The son spoke about a man who was simple and poor. He spoke about how when he was younger, he was embarrassed by his father, but as he grew older, his respect for his father grew.

The son was sorry that he only came to appreciate his father when it was "too late" but was proud that he was continuing his father's legacy by raising his children in Jerusalem where they wouldn't have a luxurious life, but a meaningful one. The son concluded his eulogy: "Dad, you didn't have much to leave behind, but you left behind EVERYTHING that matters."

This week's Torah reading begins with the commandment to Aaron and his sons to light the menorah, the seven-branched lamp in the Temple. Last week's reading was about the gifts that the princes from each of the twelve tribes brought to God. The Sages explain the connection between this week's reading and last week's portion. After watching the princes offer gifts, Aaron felt bad that he hadn't contributed anything. So God comforted him by pointing out that his descendants would light the menorah forever.

Question: Why does God highlight the menorah when there were many other duties that Aaron and his descendants would perform in the Temple? Another question: How was this "forever"? Didn't the lighting of the menorah cease after the Temples were destroyed?

The Sages explain what God meant. Centuries later, under Greek oppression, Aaron's descendants would be the ones to defeat them. You see, his descendants were the Maccabees, and their victory is remembered every year on the holiday of Hanukkah. On that holiday, we light our own menorahs, and that is how Aaron's descendants light the menorah forever!

The menorah and its lights represent spirituality, and lighting the menorah symbolizes spreading spirituality and the light of God in the darkness of this world. When God gave Aaron the job of lighting the menorah for eternity, He was telling him that through his family, God's light would be spread throughout the world and His legacy would be continued.

Sharing God's light and passing it on to the next generation is the kind of contribution that lasts forever. It's not about how much we leave behind in this world; it's about leaving behind what matters the most.

With prayers for *shalom*, peace,
Rabbi Yechiel Eckstein, May 21, 2013

Ethical Will

I leave you my unpaid debts. They are my greatest assets. Everything I own – I owe:

1. To America I owe a debt for the opportunity it gave me to be free and to be me.

2. To my parents I owe America. They gave it to me and I leave it to you. Take good care of it.

3. To the biblical tradition I owe the belief that man does not live by bread alone, nor does he live alone at all. This is also the democratic tradition. Preserve it.

4. To the six million of my people and to the thirty million other humans who died because of man's inhumanity to man, I owe a vow that it must never happen again.

5. I leave you not everything I never had, but everything I had in my lifetime: a good family, respect for learning, compassion for my fellowman, and some four-letter words for all occasions: words like "help," "give," "care," "feel," and "love."

Love, my dear grandchildren, is easier to recommend than to define. I can only tell you that like those who came before you, you will surely know when love ain't; you will also know when mercy ain't and brotherhood ain't.

The millennium will come when all the "ain'ts" shall have become all the "ises" and all the "ises" shall be for all, even for those you don't like.

Finally I leave you the years I should like to have lived so that I might possibly see whether your generation' will bring more love and peace to the world than ours did. I not only hope you will. I pray that you will.

-Sam Levenson

The Gift of Memory

Judaism should make us aware of the sacred gift of memory. We are indeed blessed by our ability to conjure up the images of past loves and glories and friendships. No one is so poor as one who suffers from forgetfulness of the soul. When our memory dies, we cease to live as rich, creative human beings. Sometimes, it is true, memory is terribly poignant. It afflicts us in moments of recent bereavement like a cutting knife, but as time passes, memory becomes also our healing balm.

Our lives are inspired and enriched by our humanly unique

capacity to recall, in the concert chamber of reminiscence, the stirring music of the lives of our beloved dead. We remember them like some gay dawn, some glorious sunrise, some striking bit of sculpture come to grace our little day on earth. To us they were life and motion imprisoned and encased transiently in flesh and blood. The example of their lives persuades us to courage and to nobility. Their personalities give us faith that the universe is not dark and somber and cruel at its heart. Religion then calls upon us to be grateful, not only for the gift of life, but for the gift of memory.

-Adapted from Rabbi Joshua Loth Liebman

The Death of a Tzaddik

As the Israelites neared the end of their forty-year trek in the wilderness, they lost two great leaders, Miriam and Aaron. While a tremendous loss for the nation, their passing had a hidden spiritual benefit.

The Torah informs us of Miriam's death immediately after enumerating the laws of the *Parah Adumah*, the red heifer whose ashes were used for purification. The Talmudic sages already wondered what connection there might be between Miriam's death and the Parah Adumah:

"Why is the death of Miriam juxtaposed to the laws of the *Parah Adumah*? This teaches that just as the *Parah Adumah* brings atonement, so too, the death of the righteous brings atonement." (Mo'ed Katan 28a).

While this connection between Miriam and the *Parah Adumah* is well known, the continuation of the same Talmudic statement, concerning the death of Aaron, is less so.

"And why is the death of Aaron juxtaposed to [the mention of] the priestly clothes? This teaches that just as the priestly clothes bring atonement, so too, the death of the righteous brings atonement."

In what way does the death of *tzaddikim* atone for the people? And why does the Talmud infer this lesson from both the *Parah Adumah* and the priestly clothes?

The principal benefit that comes from the death of *tzaddikim* is the spiritual and moral awakening that takes place after they pass away. When a *tzaddik* is alive, his acts of kindness and generosity are not always public knowledge. True *tzaddikim* do not promote themselves. On the contrary, they often take great pains to conceal their virtues and charitable deeds. It is not uncommon that we become aware of their true greatness and nobility of spirit only after they are no longer with us. Only then do we hear reports of their selfless deeds and extraordinary sensitivity, and we are inspired to emulate their ways. In this way, the positive impact of the righteous as inspiring role models increases after their death.

While stories of their fine traits and good deeds stir us to follow in their path, certain aspects of great *tzaddikim* – extraordinary erudition and scholarship, for example – are beyond the capabilities of most people to emulate. In such matters, the best we can do is to take upon ourselves to promote these qualities in our spiritual leadership, such as supporting the Torah study of young, promising scholars.

In short, the death of *tzaddikim* inspires us to imitate their personal conduct – if possible, in our own actions, and if not, by ensuring that there will be others who will fill this spiritual void.

These two methods of emulation parallel the different forms of atonement through the *Parah Adumah* and the priestly clothes. Ritual purification using *Parah Adumah* ashes was only effective when they were sprinkled on the body of the impure person; no one else could be purified in his place. This is comparable to those aspects of the *tzaddik* that are accessible to, and incumbent upon, all to emulate.

The priestly garments, on the other hand, were only worn by the *Kohanim*. It was through the service of these holy emissaries that the entire nation was forgiven. This is like those extraordinary traits of the *tzaddik* that are beyond the capabilities of most people. These qualities can be carried on only by a select few, with the support of the entire nation.

-Rabbi Abraham Isaac HaKohen Kook

Final Words

Final blessings play an important part in the Torah. At the

conclusion of Genesis, Jacob offers his words to his children –
each of the future tribes of Israel. Moses offers his final blessings
to Israel at the conclusion of Deuteronomy. When the Torah
tells us that Moses could no longer, at the end of his life, "go
in and go out" (Deut. Ch. 31) one lovely interpretation holds
that he went to the tent of each individual Israelite family and
said goodbye. When there were no more unvisited tents,
and therefore no place to go in or go out, Moses ascended the
Mountain of Nebo to die.

People who are dying sometimes feel as if they are helpless
or diminished in the eyes of others. But we will all die. How
one dies can be a powerful life lesson. Words offered to those
who will live on can be a blessing, helpful and healing.

Facing one's final moments with courage permits a grace
unequaled in more everyday settings. As the great medieval
poet, Shmuel Hanagid put it:

Take heart in time of sorrow,
Though you face death's door.
The candle flares before it dies,
And wounded lions roar

-Rabbi David Wolpe

Death Is Our Teacher

As I write this, I observe the anniversary of my mother's
death from cancer by lighting a yahrzeit (memorial) candle and
by saying Kaddish at services. I think back to my mom's last
day in the hospital for the terminally ill where she lay quiet,
unresponsive with her disquieting rasping breath. Hospice care
had graciously provided the aggressive comfort measures that
we asked for as we waited for her to die. My sister, father and
I were with her in shifts holding her hands, speaking to her of
our love and caressing her. She had just viewed for the first
time her second grandson, Gabriel, and was able to let go of
her pain and to die in peace surrounded by her family. As we
said goodbye for the night, we kissed her and left the room. My
mom had died before we arrived at the elevator. Immediately

before she expired, she exclaimed, "Mother!" as she saw her mom, according to the nurse. Viewing her newest grandson, being kissed by her family, and being reunited with deceased loved ones, paved the way for her good death.

In the Torah, Moses confronts his mortality, "And God said to Moses, Get up into this Mount Abarim, and see the land which I have given to the people of Israel. And when you have seen it, you also shall be gathered to your people..." (Numbers 27:12-13). Like my mom, Moses wanted to see the labor of his dreams, the Promised Land. After forty years of wandering and wondering if they would ever get there, God informs Moses of the verdict. Because of the sin of Meriba, he will not be able to enter, only to gaze from afar. But Moses had such a special relationship with God, that according to one Midrash, God kissed Moses and he was gathered to his people without a peep of protest. Rather than bemoaning his fate, Moses calmly accepts his finitude. He finishes his earthly responsibilities by asking God to appoint a new leader.

Moses' death in this *parasha* teaches us how to live. Death becomes a chance to do a *heshbon nefesh* (inner reckoning) as to how we live. Success may be defined as looking into your grandchildren's eyes and smiling; for Moses, it included passing on the torch of leadership to his Divinely picked successor Joshua by the laying on of hands. Only then is he prepared to die, knowing that the next generation is taken care of.

We can emulate Moses in modern times, preparing for our own deaths by attending to medical health care directives to guide our caregivers in our medical wishes; ethical wills to inspire our heirs with the values we lived; and living eulogies/ funeral instructions to help the bereaved and funeral director plan the funeral. All these preparations can help give us the peace of mind to accept death as Moses did and merit a good death. We can also use the traditional Jewish prayer for the dying, the *Viddui*, final confessional, to say good bye and let go. This may be read by the ill person or on his/her behalf. After imploring God for a *refuah shleimah*, the prayer asks God to forgive us of any sins we may have committed and to look after our loved ones. While *refuah shleimah* is frequently translated as "speedy recovery," here it can mean a healing of peace or a complete healing. While it is doubtful that the terminally ill may have a speedy recovery, if they prepare for dying after living a full life, they may merit a good death as Moses did, and die in peace with the kiss of God on their lips.

-Rabbi Eliot Baskin

Chapter Eleven

AFTERLIFE: IMAGINING A NEW EXISTENCE

Unlike many other religious traditions, Judaism has relatively little to say about the afterlife, or *olam ha-ba*, the world to come, although it has always been counted as a core belief of traditional Jewish practice. Indeed, at its beginnings, Reform Judaism rejected belief in an afterlife altogether, although modern practice recognizes a range of beliefs on this subject. Judaism has always concentrated on what we can do during our lives on this earth, the *mitzvot* we can perform here, which the dead can no longer do. As Rabbi Michael Gold notes below, "My tradition is not about getting to heaven in the next world, but creating heaven in this world." Yet the thought of loved ones entering into some kind of afterlife, or the possibility of doing so ourselves, is comforting to many. Our liturgy notes that "The dead do not praise God; those who sleep silently" (Ps. 116); this is our task on earth. But neither are they cut off from God; depending upon one's personal conception, they may be singing God's praises or forever in the holy Presence of God, or perhaps even at study in the *Yeshivah shel Ma'alah*, the study hall on high.

Death Does Not Exist

Death is non-existent. According to the Biblical legend, Adam was punished for his sin of disobedience by becoming mortal. His sin brought death as well as man's fear of death into being. But the return of the world to its source will conquer death. Every improvement of the individual or the world; every act leading toward the achievement of perfection constitutes a step toward the conquest of death by the return of the world to its original state of union with God. Death is a lie; it is an illusion. The very fact that Jewish tradition associates death with ritual uncleanliness is a symbol of its falsehood. What men call death is in reality the intensification or reinvigoration of life. The liberation from the fetters of corporeality is the indispensable means of mankind's self-renewal and the instrument of its progress. Fear of death is the universal disease of mankind, but death is terrifying and inexorable only where man is alienated from the source of his being. If sin brought death into being, *teshuvah,* man's return to the source of his being, will conquer it. The soul is not a mere appendage to the body which perishes together with the body; it is part of that undying current of vitality which returns to its source at death.

-*Samuel Hugo Bergman*

So Too Does the Soul Evolve

The process of dying is painful,
Especially if it is prolonged.
But death itself is a transition,
A transfer from here to there,
A recycling of the body and the soul.

Matter is never destroyed, only transformed.
So too does the soul evolve, higher and higher.
From instinct to inspiration, from haughtiness to holiness,

From selfishness to service, from individualism to union,
Until it returns home to the Soul of Souls –
     the *Ein Sof* – the Infinite One.

Thus is the Divine Source of Life Magnified and Sanctified.

-*Rabbi Allen S. Maller*

Feeling Their Presence

Rabbi Shoni Labovitz, in her book, "Miraculous Living" (Simon & Schuster, 1996, p. 301) describes the feeling we get when reciting Yizkor, or on any occasions when we visualize a loved one in our mind's eye.

A wise person said that prayer recited with pure intention goes beyond time, affecting those who have passed on, those who are here today, and those who are yet to be born.

I can understand this in my own experience. Sometimes I feel myself praying for people who are long gone, and I know the energy is reaching them as though they were here now. At other times, when I pray for those who are very present in my life now or those who are yet to be born, I can feel the sensation of the energy of the prayer reaching their spirits.

The Hebrew word for coffin is Aron. Aron is the same word that is used for the Holy Ark in which a Sefer Torah is housed. And it is used in another place in the Torah. When Noah builds a floating house in which to bring his family when the flood is coming, the Torah calls it an "Aron." So the Torah is called an "Aron, just as the Holy Ark in the Sanctuary, and the floating house which Noah built. The coffin is an "Aron" because, like the Holy Ark that contains the Sefer Torah, that which it contains is holy. It holds the remains of a holy being for all time.

The Aron that holds the remains of a holy person is very small. There just enough room for the person inside. Not enough room for anything but the good deeds done in this world. There is no need and no room for stocks or bonds or cash or bank accounts – these can't be used in the world where our loved ones go after death.

Maybe that's why our Tradition uses the same word for a coffin, a synagogue Ark, and Noah's floating house. And for one more reason: In some Jewish communities it is the custom to drill a hole in the bottom of the coffin to hasten the return from dust to dust. Rabbi James Ponet once wrote: Even the final "home" is not so much a sanctuary FROM the world, as an entrance into it. Let's think of our loved ones as having entered the REAL world – the world of truth – *Olam Ha-emet*.

-Adapted from Rabbi Jack Riemer and Rabbi James Ponet

Heaven and Hell

"Rabbi Bana'ah, the son of Rabbi Ulla taught, Why does it not say 'it was good' on the second day of Shabbat. Because on that day the light of hell was created." (Pesachim 54a)

At last we come to the last of these weekly spiritual messages called "A Rabbi's Guide to Being Human." Next week I will return to speaking about the weekly portion. I plan to collect the full set of these messages in one long file and make them available to anyone who wants them.

We began with the beginning of life, so we should finish with the end of life. More specifically, what happens after we leave this world? I want to respond to a question I am asked more often than any other – do Jews believe in heaven and hell? Or perhaps more specifically, do I believe in heaven and hell?

Last year on Yom Kippur I shared a story that I learned from a Buddhist monk. Buddhist stories are almost as good as Hassidic stories. There was a Buddhist monk who was considered the wisest man in the world. And there was warrior who was considered the strongest man in the world. One day the wise monk met the vicious warrior on a narrow bridge. The warrior saw him and became angry. "You think you are so wise. But I am far stronger than you. Tell me, what can you possibly teach me that I do not already know." The monk answers, "I can show you the door to hell and the door to heaven." The warrior is infuriated. He screams, "How dare you! Get out of my way before I kill you." The monk answers, "That is the door to hell." Suddenly the warrior felt bad, "I am so sorry. I guess I lost my temper." The monk said, "And that is the door to heaven."

This story is similar to another one often told. A man asks an angel to show him heaven and hell. First he is taken to hell. He sees a room full of people sitting at tables with delicious food. But everybody is crying. He notices that the people have no elbows; they cannot bend their arms. Then he is taken to heaven. Here too is a room full of people sitting at tables with delicious food. Here too the people have no elbows. But everybody is laughing and having a great time. He asks, "What is the difference?" The angel answers, "In heaven they feed each other."

The theme of both of these stories is the same. Heaven and hell are something that we create in this world. My tradition is not about getting to heaven in the next world, but creating heaven in this world. Too often we miss that urgent point.

What about the next world? We Jews speak about *Gan Eden* (Garden of Eden), the place where righteous souls go in the next world. We speak about *Gehinom* (literally "the valley of Hinom," a valley near Jerusalem where child sacrifice used to take place. That is where sinners go in the next world. But even for sinners, the maximum punishment is for one year. Rabbinic sources often wax poetic on what life is like in Gan Eden, and alternatively on the horrors of *Gehinom.* But the final description is kept deliberately vague.

Let me share my vision of what happens when we reach the next world. Imagine a child sent to the market with a grocery list and money, and he buys what he is supposed to buy. Now imagine that same child sent to the market, who buys candy and toys instead. What would it be like when each child returns home and faces his or her parents? I imagine that we are like those children sent into this world with a job to do. Suppose we did our best to fulfill our mission and do the right thing on this earth. We can face our Creator with assurance of acceptance. That is heaven. Now suppose we wasted our life, pursued meaningless pleasure, acted cruelly towards others. We face our Creator with fear and trembling. That is hell.

My tradition believes in life after death. But the key question we each must face is – when we lived did we create heaven on earth or did we create hell on earth.

-Rabbi Michael Gold

There Is No Death

"You are anxious about whether you will rise from the dead or not, but you have risen already – you rose from the dead when you were born and you didn't notice it. ... What happens to your consciousness? Your consciousness, yours, not anyone else's. And now look. You in others are yourself, your soul. This is what you are. This is what your consciousness has breathed and lived on and enjoyed throughout your life. And what now? You have always been in others and you will remain in others. And what does it matter to you if later on it is called your memory? This will be you – the you that enters the future and becomes a part of it. And now one last point. There is nothing to worry about. There is no death."

-Boris Pasternak, Doctor Zhivago

Like a Lost Vessel

"Forgotten from the heart like the dead, I have become like a lost vessel."

-Psalms 31:13

Hunted by his enemies, David felt betrayed and abandoned.

Why did David describe his sense of isolation and loneliness as being like a "lost vessel"? In what way are the dead like lost objects?

The Sages learned from here that, in some aspects, our emotional ties to loved ones are like our ties to possessions. When an object is lost, it takes a full year before one loses all hope of recovering it. So, too, The dead are only forgotten from the heart after twelve months have passed (Berachot 58b).

For this reason, when seeing a friend after a year has passed with no contact, one should recite the blessing which praises God as "*Mehaiyei ha-meitim*" – "Who revives the dead." For us, it is as if our friend has come back to life.

Of course, we remember those whom we love even after a year has passed. The searing pain of loss, however, is experienced primarily during that first year.

What function do these heartrending emotions of grief and mourning serve? Would it not be better if we could immediately reconcile ourselves to the loss, without having to undergo a lengthy process of bereavement?

If a certain trait is ingrained in the human soul, it must have some basis in reality. There must be some aspect of the world – if not in its current state, then in a future, repaired state – that is reflected by this characteristic of the soul.

If death were truly a case of irrevocable loss, we would not mourn the passing of those we love for such a long time period. It would serve no purpose. The very fact that these feelings of profound bereavement and loss are a universal aspect of human nature indicates that death is not an immutable state.

The psalmist's comparison of the dead with lost articles reinforces this conclusion. When we lose an object, why do we not immediately give up hope of recovering it? Because we know the lost object still exists; we just don't know its precise

◆ 179 ◆

location. In fact, it is this very sense of loss that spurs our efforts to search for and recover the object.

The lengthy period of mourning after the death of a loved one indicates that, for humanity as a whole, the future promises a remedy for death. But unlike lost objects, this process will be through Divine means.

"Then you will know that I am God – when I open up your graves and lead you up out of your graves" (Ezekiel 37:13).

Since this *tikkun* will ultimately transpire, even now we refuse to accept death as an expected – although tragic – occurrence. Rather, we relate to death like the loss of a highly prized object which we still hope to recover.

A lost vessel is not truly gone, just missing with regard to its owner. So too, the soul is eternal; death merely places it outside our reach. The lengthy passage of time during which we long for that which appears unrecoverable is a sign that there is indeed hope. Thus the prophets foretold a future era, when the dead will be resurrected to life:

"Your dead will come to life, My corpses will rise up. Awaken and sing, you who dwell in the dust." (Isaiah 26:19)

-*Rabbi Abraham Isaac HaKohen Kook*

Chapter Twelve

BEFORE IT'S TOO LATE –
"GIVE ME MY ROSES NOW"

Don't strew me with roses after I'm dead.
When Death claims the light of my brow,
No flowers of life will cheer me: instead
You may give me my roses now!

-Thomas F. Healey

Perhaps you have picked up this book because you have lost someone dear to you, and you are wondering about the future, and how you might respond to other losses that, sadly, are a part of the human condition. Or perhaps your loved ones are old, or ill, but still alive and with you. What can you do for them?

If there is anything that the experience of a death teaches us, it is that we must live now, in this moment, not in tomorrow or the next day or the next year. We, or those we love, might not see those times. But we are here now, and there is much we can offer each other now. We need never wish that we had told Mom how much we love her, or Dad how much we enjoyed studying or riding in the car with him. We need never berate ourselves for putting off telling our friends how much their friendship means to us. If we live now, we will tell them what is in our hearts, and do the things we want to do with them, in this moment, not in some future that might never arrive.

If we only have today, what will our priorities be?

There Is Nothing More Precious Than Time

In "The Caine Mutiny", Herman Wouk has the father of the hero of the book, Willie, write a letter to his son. He advises him, "Remember this, if you can – there is nothing, nothing more precious than time. You probably feel you have a measureless supply of it, but you haven't. Wasted hours destroy your life just as surely at the beginning as at the end – only at the end it becomes more obvious."

Is there a word of kindness that we need to speak to someone? Is there a letter or a phone call that we have to make? Is there a word of forgiveness or of prayer that we need to offer? Or, is there some major change that we have again postponed making? We don't know if we have tomorrow. All that we have is *hayom* – today.

Here are just a few changes that I am planning to make in the way that I use my time in the coming new year:

I plan to spend more time with my family

I plan to spend more time studying.

I plan to spend less time worrying.

I plan to spend more time trying new things.

How are you planning to use your time differently this year?

-*Rabbi Hayim Herring*

Keep the Toys, I'll Take the Time

Sometimes it takes a child to remind us of the proper priorities of life. Recently I officiated at a memorial service for a young parent. Speaking to his only child, a boy of eleven years old, I asked him what he remembered most about his father. He thought for a moment and said, "He bought me a lot of toys and spent a lot of time with me. Rabbi, you can have the toys, but I want the time."

I think of the story of a woman who lost her home during Hurricane Katrina in New Orleans. A reporter interviewed her and noticed she was smiling. "How can you still smile when you home has been taken from you." She looked at him with a big smile and said, "I have learned in my life not to cry for things that don't cry for me."

How gladly all of us would return the things to retrieve the treasure of time. The present quickly becomes the past in that mortal time clock of life. I vividly remember a great preacher teacher Rabbi Baruch Silverstein z"l, who served as President of the New York Board of Rabbis. He wrote a masterful sermon entitled, Unclaimed and Uncollected in which he described those bank accounts that revert to the state because no stakeholder has come forward in seven years. He wondered how many of us do the same thing, allowing time to be lost because we did not claim it.

Some choices in life are difficult; others should be easy. "Keep the toys, I'll take the time."

-Rabbi Joseph Potasnik

The End of Life

"The dead do not praise God."

-Psalms 115:17

The Jewish year is winding down. And so is this series on being human. After the holidays, I will return to writing about the portion of the week. We began this series with the beginning of life. Therefore, it seems appropriate that we end this series with the end of life.

The Welch poet Dylan Thomas famously wrote the words "Do not go gentle into that good night; Rage, rage against the dying of the light." He is passionately reiterating an idea as old as the Bible – "Therefore choose life." (Deut. 30:19) The World-to-Come is not a better world. This world is where the action is. Yet, as much as we rage against the dying of the light, each of us must die. Entropy is the way of the earth. All material things including our own bodies must break down. The Bible says it best, "There is a time to be born and a time to die." (Ecc. 3:2) How we deal with the end of our life reflects how we feel about life.

The Bible, reflecting a deep mythic truth, teaches that we are not meant to live forever. God drives humanity from the Garden of Eden so that we will not eat from the Tree of Life and gain immortality. (See Gen. 3:22-23) The story goes on to teach, "The Lord said, My breath shall not abide in man forever, since he too is flesh; let the days allowed him be one hundred and twenty years." (Gen. 6:3) From this passage came the Jewish tradition that whenever we mention someone's age, we add the words "until a hundred and twenty."

The book of Psalms is a bit more realistic about the number

of years we are given. "The days of our years are but seventy, and if given the strength eighty." (Psalms 90:10) Today with new medical techniques, more of us are living longer and longer. (Of course, that creates problems of its own; how can society care for the increasing number of elderly people?) But none of us will live forever. How ought we to deal with the end of our lives?

There is an insight in a simple Jewish ritual. When a man dies, he is buried in his tallit (prayer shawl). I suppose today, with more women wearing a tallit, the same law will apply to women. But the custom is to make a cut in one of the fringes, making the tallit not kosher. It symbolizes the idea that when we are gone, we can no longer keep God's commandments. When we leave this bodily existence, we can no longer do God's work. Or as the Psalmist said, "The dead cannot praise God." Our tradition says "choose life" to teach us that we should continue to perform *mitzvot*, to do God's work, as long as we are alive on this earth. When we are gone, we cannot do them any longer.

What can someone do towards the end of their life? Here Jewish tradition also has an answer. There is a practice reaching back to the Bible of leaving an ethical will. A will usually deals with how one's property will be dispersed. An ethical will is not about property; it is about values. What values do we want to leave to our descendants? What can we teach them on how to live their lives? What do we want them to remember us? An ethical will is a wonderful way to continue to have an effect on the world after we are gone, by leaving wisdom to those who will follow in our footsteps.

Another important practice for one nearing the end is to make clear arrangements for what one wants after they are gone. I perform too many funerals for people who left their family scrambling to make final arrangements, often with no clear guidelines. I have sadly buried parents of young children who never bothered to buy insurance so their children would be properly cared for. I have mediated family conflicts among survivors. It is a great gift to make one's thoughts clear while still in this world.

Finally, I am a strong believer in hospice. Hospice teaches

that every moment of life including the end should be lived as fully as possible. We should live our last days not in a hospital enduring aggressive medical actions to extend our lives. Rather we should live pain-free, surrounded by the people we love, with no heroic measures. To die with dignity is the final step in living with dignity.

-Rabbi Michael Gold

Time Out – Life is Temporary

I don't wear a watch. I haven't worn one in years; not since I read a book on how overly time-conscious people drive themselves to an early grave. But lately I've been reconsidering. The watch is designed by David Kendrick of Berkshire, New York.

A little over a year ago, Mr. Kendrick received a patent for a "Life Expectancy Timepiece." The watch contains a tiny computer into which you feed your age, medical history, life-style, eating habits and exercise regimens. The watch then uses actuarial data to compute your life expectancy and begins counting to zero.

Imagine walking down the street and someone asks you the time. You glance at your watch and say: "Oh, about 37 years, 110 days, 21 hours, 4 minutes and 42 seconds until I die." Isn't that more interesting than saying "3:45?"

I don't need to wear the hour on my wrist. There are clocks everywhere; but being able to glance down and watch my life ticking away before my eyes, now that's something!

Some of you may be thinking: "God, how depressing!" On the contrary, being reminded that my life is temporary is incredibly liberating: "You mean I won't have to stand in line at the Post Office forever? Fantastic!"

Let me tell you five ways Mr. Kendrick's watch would affect my life.

First, it would shock me. "Whoa! You mean I've only got this much time left?" Knowing I'm going to die in 37 years, 110 days, 21 hours, 4 minutes and 42 seconds (41 seconds, 40 seconds, 39 seconds). In the face of death life becomes awesomely simple: acts of love and kindness, justice, and compassion are what count rather than the acts of revenge and one-upmanship that occupy most of our lives. In the face of this awesome simplicity I would love more and lie less.

Second, Mr. Kendrick's timepiece would focus my attention on doing rather than feeling.

Feelings are fleeting, uncontrollable and unstable. Anger, love, sadness, joy trip over each other as they fit into and out of consciousness. Seeing the transience of my life-would make the transience of my feelings even clearer. When we try to lock certain feelings in and other feelings out we live in constant frustration. By focusing attention on doing rather than feeling, I can make my life constructive, productive, effortful. Effort often leads to success, and success often brings positive feelings. Waiting to feel before we do is waiting to fail. Doing alone brings success. The old adage: Those who can do, do is backward. The truth is: Those who can do, can.

Third, Mr. Kendrick's watch would focus my attention on the present. So much of our time is spent dwelling on the past or dreaming about the future. Both past and future are figments of the imagination distracting us from now. All there is, is now and here and the work of the moment. Which brings me back to the fourth impact of this timepiece: ordinariness.

I'm nothing special: just a temporary animation of cells. I am simply God's way of getting things done. Do you want to know why you were born. To pick up the trash, to do the laundry, to parent a child, to feed the hungry, to visit the sick, to care for an aged parent, to brush your teeth. You were born to do whatever life gives you to do right now.

The illusion of specialness is at the root of so many adult problems. We are wrong. As Hillel taught: "If I am not for myself who will be for me, but if I am only for myself what am I? And if not now when?" Taking care of me requires taking care of you. What is a person who is only for the self? An aging adolescent perpetually seeking the inner child.

Lastly, Mr. Kendrick's watch would help me relax. Rather than feeling I've got to cram my years with meaningful experience, I would experience the years as they come. So many of us are convinced that the way our lives should have turned out is somehow other than the way they did turn out.

Why? Why do we deserve other than what we got? Why think we deserve anything?

Here I've got 37 years, 21 hours, 4 minutes and 42 seconds to go and life is what it is for the moment. And if I don't like what I've got I can do something to change it; do something other than whine and dream and dwell on why I deserve better. Most of us are unhappy that we didn't get what we imagine we "deserve." Maybe we did. Scary thought, isn't it?

I think Mr. Kendrick's watch would be a lifesaver for me, and many others like me. Unfortunately, the watch is not yet on the market. Too bad. I'd buy one. Better still, I'd wear it. And the next time someone would ask me "What time is it?" I'd say "Thanks!"

-Rabbi Rami M. Shapiro

Don't Wait Till It's Too Late

Thomas Carlyle lived from 1795 until 1881. He was a Scot essayist and historian. During his lifetime he became one of the world's greatest writers. But he was a human and humans make mistakes.

On October 17, 1826, Carlyle married his secretary Jane Welsh. She was an intelligent, attractive and somewhat temperamental daughter of a well-to-do doctor. They had their quarrels and misunderstandings, but still loved each other dearly. After their marriage, Jane continued to serve as his secretary. After several years of marriage, Jane became ill. Being a hard worker, Carlyle became so absorbed in his writings that he let Jane continue working for several weeks after she became ill. She had cancer, and it was one of the slow growing kind. Finally, she became confined to her bed. Although Carlyle loved her dearly, he very seldom found time to stay with her long. He was busy with his work.

When Jane died they carried her to the cemetery for the service. The day was a miserable day. It was raining hard and the mud was deep. Following the funeral Carlyle went back to his home. He was taking it pretty hard. He went up the stairs to Jane's room and sat down in the chair next to her bed. He sat there thinking about how little time he had spent with her and wishing so much he had a chance to do it differently. Noticing her diary on a table beside the bed, he picked up and began to read in it.

Suddenly he seemed shocked. He saw it. There, on one page, she had written a single line. "Yesterday he spent an hour with me and it was like heaven; I love him so." Something dawned on him that he had not noticed before. He had been too busy to notice that he meant so much to her. He thought of all the times he had gone about his work without thinking about and noticing her.

Then Carlyle turned the page in the diary. There he noticed written some words that broke his heart. "I have listened all day to hear his steps in the hall, but now it is late and I guess he won't come today." Carlyle read a little more in the book. Then he threw it down and ran out of the house. Some of his friends found him at the grave, his face buried in the mud. His eyes were red from weeping. Tears continued to roll down his cheeks. He kept repeating over and over again, "If I had only known, if I had only known." But it was too late for Carlyle. She was dead.

After Jane's death, Carlyle made little attempt to write again. The historian said he lived another 15 years, "weary, bored and a partial recluse."

I tell the story with the hope that you will not make the same mistake. While our loved ones must have the money we make to live, it is the love we have that they really want. Give it now before it is too late.

-Unknown

Remembering to Say Thank You

When I look back upon my early days, I am stirred by the thought of the number of people whom I have to thank for what they gave me or what they were to me. At the same time, I am haunted by an oppressive consciousness of the little gratitude I really showed them while I was young. How many of them have said farewell to life without my having made clear to them what it means to me to receive from them so much kindness or so much care! Many a time have I, with a feeling of shame, said

quietly to myself over a grave the words which my mouth ought
to have spoken to the departed while he was still in the flesh.

-Albert Schweitzer

I, May I Rest In Peace

I, may I rest in peace – I, who am still living, say,
May I have peace in the rest of my life.
I want peace right now while I'm still alive.
I don't want to wait like that pious man
     who wished for one leg of the golden chair of Paradise,
I want a four-legged chair right here, a plain wooden chair.
I want the rest of my peace now.
I have lived out my life in wars of every kind: battle without
     and within, close combat, face-to-face, my enemy face.
Wars with the old weapons – sticks and stones,
     blunt axe, words, dull ripping knife, love and hate,
     and wars with newfangled weapons – machine gun,
     missile, words, land mines exploding, love and hate.
I don't want to fulfill my parents' prophecy that life is war.
I want peace with all my body and all my soul.
Rest me in peace.

-Yehuda Amichai
Chana Bloch and Chana Kronfeld

The Time Is Now

If you are ever going to love me,
Love me now, while I can know
The sweet and tender feelings
Which from true affection flow.

Love me now
While I am living.

Do not wait until I'm gone
And then have it chiseled in marble,
Sweet words on ice-cold stone.
If you have tender thoughts of me,

Please tell me now.
If you wait until I am sleeping,
Never to awaken,
There will be death between us
And I won't hear you then.

So, if you love me, even a little bit,
Let me know it while I am living
So I can treasure it.

-Unknown

Burying a Friend Younger than Me

Today I buried a man who had everything to live for. He was youthful and handsome with a beautiful young family. He stemmed from prosperity and had charisma and an electrifying personality.

He had been through a rough patch.

Had he lived to see his fortieth birthday – which he died just shy of – I would have shared with him what I learned from that milestone.

On the night that I turned 40 I stayed awake waiting for "it" to hit me like a freight train. The "it" was the promised wisdom from the words of the sages: At forty a man becomes wise.

I had thought myself smart but not wise and I knew the famous Jewish saying about the difference between the two: the smart man can extricate himself from a situation into which the wise man would never have gotten himself into in the first place.

I wanted to be wise. I wanted the great secret of life, the nugget of wisdom that was going to make it all better. The granule of knowledge passed on from the ancients that would make life simple, smooth, and effortless. I wanted the esoteric secret that render life seamless, bereft of challenge and struggle.

It did not come.

Not that night, not that year, and not the next year. I was sorely disappointed. I felt cheated. I told my wife that the wisdom did not arrive. That I still did not have the answers to life's great questions. Life for me was still a struggle.

And then, at about age 44, it finally happened. It arrived.

The wisdom I had always waited for, the secret that had long eluded me.

It was this.

There is no great wisdom, there is no great secret, that will ever make life's struggle easier. The essence of wisdom is to know that we will never know. Life will always be challenging. It would always demand great effort.

For each and every one of us it would be a struggle to be happily married. It would be challenging to raise good and purposeful children. It would be a battle to maintain healthy self-esteem. It would be a struggle to reject corrosive values.

It would never get easier and the struggle was worth it.

The ancient Rabbis said that an olive releases its oil only when pressed, a grape produces wine when squeezed.

But my friend was too young to hear that message. The struggle too painful, the road too rough.

He too sought the means by which to alleviate the struggle but found it in radically different way. And there but for the grace of God.

The funeral of a young person renders many lessons but none greater than this: go home and hug your children. Tell them that amid our attempts to hammer and chisel them into perfection we do so knowing all the while that they are already perfect.

I called my daughter who's studying at University. "Baby girl, if I found a genie in a bottle on a beach who would give me unlimited power to change anything in the world, I wouldn't change a single thing about you."

Our children so often hear the opposite message. That we love them but we want to modify things about them. That they're great kids, but why did you get a "C". That you're worthy, but you can always be more deserving.

Once one of my children's teachers called to complain that our son was speaking during class. He asked me to reprimand him. I called my son into my office. "Do you know why I want to speak to you?" My son responded, "Yes, because the teacher called to complain about me and said I wasn't behaving in class."

"That's not right," I said. "I called you into my office to tell you that I love you. That I don't say it enough. That you're the most amazing son and you give me endless pride. That no matter what you do I will always love you ... And by the way, don't interrupt your teacher in class."

Go home and tell your wives how beautiful they are. Make them feel valued and appreciated. Give them your attention and limitless affection. Go home and tell your husbands that they're not just ATMs. That they're cherished and admired for more than what they provide.

Honor and visit your parents. Love and treasure your grandparents.

Let us never allow loss to be our teacher. Let us learn to love and laugh not because life is short but rather because it is infinitely precious.

-Rabbi Shmuley Boteach

ACKNOWLEDGMENTS

We would like to acknowledge the following publishers and individuals for permission to reprint excerpts included in this book.

Fear Not Death by permission of Adena Greenberg

Is It Really the End? by permission of Adena Greenberg

Feeling the Sun from Both Sides by permission of Adena Greenberg

The Greatest Compensation by permission of Adena Greenberg

God is Now Here by permission of Adena Greenberg

A Thought for the New Year: The Holiness of Time by permission of Adena Greenberg

Just in Time by permission of Steve Goodier-http://www.LifeSupportSystem.com

When Someone Grieves by permission of Steve Goodier-http://www.LifeSupportSystem.com

Finding the Right Words by permission of Steve Goodier-http://www.LifeSupportSystem.com

Who Rekindles Your Light? by permission of Steve Goodier-http://www.LifeSupportSystem.com

When Suffering Visits by permission of Steve Goodier-http://www.LifeSupportSystem.com

Finding the Way Out of Bagamoyo by permission of Steve Goodier-http://www.LifeSupportSystem.com

Celebrating My Scars by permission of Steve Goodier-http://www.LifeSupportSystem.com

Chasing A Dream by permission of Steve Goodier-http://www.LifeSupportSystem.com

We're Stronger Than We Think by permission of Steve Goodier-http://www.LifeSupportSystem.com

A Decision I Must Make Everyday by permission of Steve Goodier-http://www.LifeSupportSystem.com

Memory- Your Greatest Treasure by permission of Steve Goodier-http://www.LifeSupportSystem.com

Viddui- Final Confession by permission of Rabbi Vicky Hollander

Get a Life by permission of Rabbi Jeffrey Salkin

A Holy Place by permission of Rabbi Amy Eilberg

Voice of the Soul by permission of Blair P. Grubb, MD

To What End? by permission of Rabbi Margaret Holub

The Metaphysics of Mourning by permission of Rabbi Margaret Holub

Reflections Upon the New Year by permission of Rabbi David J. Wolpe

The Fire in Our Lives by permission of Rabbi David J. Wolpe

A Time for Silence by permission of Rabbi David J. Wolpe

The Process of Mourning by permission of Rabbi David J. Wolpe

What of the Things That Die While We are Still Alive? by permission of Rabbi David J. Wolpe

Stand Up Straight by permission of Rabbi David J. Wolpe

The Shape of Human Hearts by permission of Rabbi David J. Wolpe

The Masterpiece of Sorrow by permission of Rabbi David J. Wolpe

To Hold with Open Arms by permission of Rabbi David J. Wolpe

An Answer to Evil by permission of Rabbi David J. Wolpe

The Secret of the Kaddish by permission of Rabbi David J. Wolpe

Take Your Time by permission of Rabbi David J. Wolpe

Bittersweet by permission of Rabbi David J. Wolpe

My Mother and Helen Keller by permission of Rabbi David J. Wolpe

Overcoming by permission of Rabbi David J. Wolpe

Our Parents and Grandparents-They are Still with Us by permission of Rabbi David J. Wolpe

Final Words by permission of Rabbi David J. Wolpe

Notice You're Alive by permission of Carl A. Hammerschlag, MD

Entering the Real World by permission of Rabbi Jack Riemer and Rabbi James Ponet

What Have We Lost, and What Do We Still Have? by permission of Rabbi Jack Riemer

Feeling Their Presence by permission of Rabbi Jack Riemer and Rabbi James Ponet

Nothing to Fear by permission of Rabbi Abraham J. Twerski

Dying a Good Death by permission of Rabbi Yehuda Appel

God Has Given, God Has Taken-May the Name of God Be Blessed. Reprinted by permission of the author. © 2006 by Robert Scheinberg

A Letter to My Niece about Death by permission of Sandra Shaw Friedman

Driving Sorrow Out of Your Life by permission of Rabbi Steven Carr Reuben

Together-We Can Stand Anything by permission of Rabbi Dannel I. Schwartz

Good Grief. © by Rabbi Kenneth L. Cohen

Perspective by permission of Rabbi Philip Rice

Love and Consolation by permission of Rabbi Marc D. Angel. Reprinted from Jewishideas.org

When We Can't Understand by permission of Rabbi Yechiel Eckstein. Excerpted with permission from Holy Land Moments with Rabbi Yechiel Eckstein, © 2013-2014, the International Fellowship of Christians and Jews ®. A copy of the full text can be obtained from The Fellowship, 30 N. LaSalle Street, Suite 4300, Chicago, IL 60602-2584

How Long the Night? by permission of Rabbi Yechiel Eckstein. Excerpted with permission from Holy Land Moments with Rabbi Yechiel Eckstein, © 2013-2014, the International Fellowship of Christians and Jews ®. A copy of the full text can be obtained from The Fellowship, 30 N. LaSalle Street, Suite 4300, Chicago, IL 60602-2584

Passing the Torch by permission of Rabbi Yechiel Eckstein. Excerpted with permission from Holy Land Moments with Rabbi Yechiel Eckstein, © 2013-2014, the International Fellowship of Christians and Jews ®. A copy of the full text can be obtained from The Fellowship, 30 N. LaSalle Street, Suite 4300, Chicago, IL 60602-2584

Let There Be Light by permission of Rabbi Zelig Pliskin. Reproduced from "Serenity" by Rabbi Zelig Pliskin with permission of the copyright holders, ArtScroll / Mesorah Publications, Ltd.

Moving On: When Kaddish Ends by permission of Rabbi Gerald Skolnik. Reprinted by permission of the Jewish Week of New York

The Minyan by permission of Rabbi Philip Scheim

How to Remember Loved Ones When You Can't Say Kaddish by permission of Rabbi Susan Fendrick. © Susan P. Fendrick

In the Year of Mourning by permission of Gary Rosenblatt. Reprinted by permission of the Jewish Week of New York

From Death to Life, From Darkness to Light From Darkness to Light by permission of Rabbi Edward Feinstein, Valley Beth Shalom, Encino, CA

Gam Zeh Ya-Avor-This Too Will Pass by permission of Rabbi Edward Feinstein, Valley Beth Shalom, Encino, CA

God is a Verb from God is a Verb: Kabbalah and the Practice of Mystical Judaism by permission of Rabbi David A. Cooper

Living for Their Dreams by permission of Rabbi Harold Kushner

Limnot Yamenu Ken Hoda by permission of Rabbi Hillel E. Silverman

Unetaneh Tokef: There is No Tomorrow by permission of Rabbi Mark B. Greenspan

The Broken Jar by permission of Rabbi Ilana Grinblat

Learning to Be Violins by permission of Rabbi Dr. Edgar J. Weinsberg

Yizkor by permission of Rabbi David Gutterman

Making the Most of Life by permission of Rabbi Stephan O. Parnes. © 2007 Stephan O. Parnes

No Petitioner Ever Succeeded in Ransoming Anything from the Captivity of Yesterday by permission of Rabbi Jonathan Wittenberg

On Loss: Ten Lessons from Sheryl Sandberg's Facebook Post by permission of Dr. Afshine Emrani

From Beyond the Grave- Our Loved Ones Reached Out and Touched Us by permission of Rabbi Michael Gold

Heaven and Hell by permission of Rabbi Michael Gold

The End of Life by permission of Rabbi Michael Gold

A Yizkor Guided Imagery Exercise by permission of Rabbi David Woznica

Names Written in Our Hearts by permission of Rabbi Matthew Simon

Memory to Touch a Name by permission of Rabbi Matthew Simon

Father by permission of Menachem Z. Rosensaft. © Menachem Z. Rosensaft

The Family Reunion by permission of Rabbi Arnold M. Goodman

A Mother's Crown by permission of Rabbi Bernhard Rosenberg

When All That's Left is Love by permission of Rabbi Allen S. Maller

So Too Does the Soul Evolve... by permission of Rabbi Allen S. Maller

Death is Our Teacher by permission of Rabbi Eliot J. Baskin

There is Nothing More Precious than Time by permission of Rabbi Hayim Herring

Keep the Toys, I'll Take the Time by permission of Rabbi Joseph Potasnik

74939047R00122

Made in the USA
San Bernardino, CA
22 April 2018